Individual
homes
GUIDE

The Daily Telegraph

Individual

homes

GUIDE

Building Your Own Home

SECOND EDITION

EDITED BY TOM ROWLAND

KOGAN
PAGE

The rules and regulations governing land and property purchase and other associated topics covered in this book are constantly being reviewed and changed. Kogan Page Limited, *The Daily Telegraph* and the authors cannot assume legal responsibility for the accuracy of any particular statement in this work. No responsibility for loss or damage occasioned to any person acting or refraining from action as a result of the material in this publication can be accepted by the authors or publishers.

First published in 1993
Second edition 1994

Apart from any fair dealing for the purposes of research or private study, or criticism or review, as permitted under the Copyright, Designs and Patents Act, 1988, this publication may only be reproduced, stored or transmitted, in any form or by any means, with the prior permission in writing of the publishers, or in the case of reprographic reproduction in accordance with the terms of licences issued by the Copyright Licensing Agency. Enquiries concerning reproduction outside those terms should be sent to the publishers at the undermentioned address:

Kogan Page Limited
120 Pentonville Road
London N1 9JN

© Tom Rowland and contributors 1993, 1994

British Library Cataloguing in Publication Data

A CIP record for this book is available from the British Library.

ISBN 0–7494–1243–7

Typeset by DP Photosetting, Aylesbury, Bucks
Printed in England by Clays Ltd, St Ives plc

We started with cheese soufflé and moved on to the British Coal.

THE BEST FIRES BURN WITH BRITISH COAL

CONTENTS

Before you build your DREAM HOME

visit the factory

Y ou can now buy the home you've always dreamed of – at a price and quality you never thought possible.

Whatever size or design you may be considering, Berg Hus triple glazed, Swedish specification, energy saving homes, provide you with the very highest levels of style, comfort and economy.

From the smallest modern home to a Tudor style mansion, each is individually architect designed and made to exacting standards at our purpose built factory.

Why not visit the factory and see for yourself how much we put into your home – or alternatively, send for our FREE 'Art of Fine Housebuilding' colour brochure *today*.

CHAPTER 1

THE IMPOSSIBLE DREAM

TOM ROWLAND

Tom Rowland is the property correspondent of *The Daily Telegraph*. He broadcasts on design, architecture and the property market; his previous books include *The Channel Tunnel: How to Sink a Fortune* and *The Inmos Saga*, a study of British technology policy in the 1970s and 1980s.

In most of Europe and North America a large proportion of middle-class home-owners have built their own houses. That is not to say that they insert the cement between the bricks themselves – although a few do – but they commission and have a hand in the design of houses built to their own specification on a parcel of land they have found.

The practice has become far more unusual in Britain, where most new houses are put up by volume builders. When offered a choice, many of those who could afford to build themselves opt for life in a draughty period house, even if the age of staffing eighteenth- and nineteenth-century domestic buildings in the way they were designed to operate has long gone, and it also costs a fortune in heating bills to make the place comfortable.

There are signs that the fashion is changing. The latest figures show that around one in three detached houses built in Britain last year were completed by individual home-builders.

Because new houses are zero-rated for Value Added Tax individual home-builders can be accurately tracked statistically when they claim their VAT back. The latest figures from Customs and Excise show that in the year 1992/93 around 10,000 private claims were made. That figure can be increased by at least 5000 to account for people who commission their own home but employ a builder/contractor to manage the project and do not make the claim themselves.

Other statistics show that last year there were 45,000 detached houses completed in Britain. Although the overall number of houses being built was down, this figure of one individual project to every two conventional ones is the highest ever. If the trend can be sustained, we should eventually fall into the same building pattern as the rest of the EC and the United States.

There have been enormous advances in building technology in the past few years; it is now possible to build a home of your own with relative ease, and without bankrupting yourself. Changing attitudes in planning departments and building societies mean that you are also less likely to end up building an uninspiring brick box.

With a little good advice and good taste you can design and build a home which is a pleasing piece of architecture, which can be heated and run at a fraction of the cost of a conventional house and which uses environmentally friendly green materials where appropriate. It will also be tailormade to meet the special needs of your family.

Individual house building covers a wide spectrum, from putting up log cabins on a shoestring to commissioning the finest architects money can buy to build you a palace. On the surface, the different sections of that spectrum have little in common beyond attracting individualists who refuse to take what is offered by builders and estate agents who inform them that it is the only housing available. But those who intend to commission an architect to manage a project from start to finish do have to deal with many of the same problems as those who intend to do at least some of the work for themselves, or to buy one of the excellent package houses now available.

Finding a site and getting planning permission in a spot where you actually want to live is still a difficult process in the UK, but for the persistent there is a great deal of help and advice available to ease the path

0800 010 100

By ringing this number, you will be put in touch with our nationwide network of Shell Distributors.

Each one is qualified to give you sound advice about the heating needs of your planned house.

Shell Distributors will be delighted to discuss with you a wide range of topics: system design, boiler types, relative costs of fuels, regulations and standards, commissioning, warranty and maintenance.

For many individual home builders, oil central heating is becoming the natural choice: cost-effective and technically advanced.

Oil, the cheapest automatic fuel, matches or exceeds the performance of other fuels in standard or condensing boilers.

One number, many solutions
0800 010 100

Technical advice from your local Shell Distributor

through the bureaucratic nightmare which is the British planning process. With some strategic advice, and a little good luck, you can significantly increase your chances of finding a good building plot.

It has become easier to finance a house-building project, but there are special problems and lending institutions need to be approached with care although, if treated correctly, they are keen to attract business that is seen as far more stable and a better risk than the marginal slice of the first-time buyer market has turned out to be.

Buying land is not the same as buying a finished house and it pays to understand the basics of the legal process. There are extra pitfalls to be avoided when buying a site, but if you know what to watch out for the chances of getting badly burned are greatly reduced.

And no matter how 'hands-off' or 'hands-on' you decide to be, when it comes to the actual building of your new home you are inevitably going to have to negotiate with a whole list of outsiders, and then manage the building process. Individual home-builders need to know how to deal with an army of bureaucrats, professionals and crafts people if they are to complete their project successfully.

This book originated with a series of seminars I organised for the first *Daily Telegraph* Individual Homes Show. Its aim is to give those considering starting on the path of building themselves a new home some of the basic guidance and advice they will need.

It is not intended as a handbook with which a house can be completed, but it does outline the issues involved in getting a project under way, and will be of use to the small but hardy band of people who each year set out to build a home from scratch as well as the growing number who hire in skills and help from outside.

CHANGES IN BRITISH PATTERNS

In Britain, the bulk of new houses are still put up by speculative builders, those heroic men who go out and buy a field, fill it with more or less identical brick houses and then set about attracting buyers.

The reasons for this different situation in Britain compared to most of the rest of the EC and to the United States are complex:

- Historically, there is a long tradition of successful speculative building in Britain which goes back to all of those splendid Georgian terraces.

- Financially, for a long time it was difficult to match or beat the prices of the volume builders.
- Once the main elements of our gloriously cumbersome planning system were in place, the big boys had the pick of all the best sites because big-scale development looks so much neater to the bureaucratic eye.

If we were to do a little trend spotting, then, during the rest of the 1990s, that fixation with the old and the ready-made is likely to change.

For economic and practical reasons, going it alone is becoming a realistic option for an increasing number of people who just a few years ago would not have seriously considered getting themselves embroiled in a building project.

The conspiracy between the builders and buyers of off-the-peg houses has been badly eroded by the unprecedented house price declines of the early 1990s. The key to this contract was that buyers were always prepared to pay a borrowed fortune for a bland and often uninspired product, in the confident expectation that they would have made even more of a fortune when they came to sell.

Its very uniformity was a plus point, making a house easy to price and sell, and the size of the investment for each purchaser had, until recently, acted as a natural damper on innovation or change. Why take risks when anyone who bought a modest new house in the early 1980s was almost certain to make more from selling than they took home in pay during the intervening three or four years?

Take away the potential for huge capital gains as well as the option to move quickly and there is an incentive for more buyers to spend time and effort getting a house the way they want it. They are going to be living there for a very long time.

It is a model that can be seen in Germany where there is a different tradition, whereby it is solid citizens in their thirties and forties who are the first-time buyers. They plan to live for a decade or more in their chosen spot, not the maximum of 36 months which a much younger first timer of late 1980s Britain hoped to spend before moving on.

In the United States you went out, found a spot and started building a homestead if you wanted a house. The idea is deeply embedded in the culture.

In Britain, where land is in far shorter supply and every square inch of it is covered by restrictive planning regulations, that has not been a sensible option for years. But, in an age when Western Europe has a growing surplus of agricultural land, the planning regime is being liberalised and it will become easier in the future to find plots for single houses, not more difficult.

Local authorities now all have structure plans which designate the use to which all land can be put, but in 1991 the Government made some important and little understood alterations to the planning system. This now operates on the principle that, for most areas, there should be a presumption in favour of allowing a development to go ahead, unless convincing objections can be demonstrated.

That does not mean that it will be possible to get permission to put a house in the centre of any field you might want to buy. It is still the local authority which grants permission, and it is supposed to stick to its structure plan.

But there is bound to be a change in attitudes on even the most intransigent planning committees. When fields can be seen transformed into golf courses or growing cultivated crops of purple wild flowers instead of food crops, and the old barn has been converted into a house, there is going to be less objection to the idea of somebody building a well-designed modern house nearby. And not before time.

Even in the densely populated south east of England, only around 11 per cent of the land is actually developed. The rest is tangled in the spaghetti of planning regulations preventing movement in any direction, while land prices have spiralled to such an extent that many people consequently cannot afford any kind of home, be it one that is built for them or one they have a hand in building themselves.

This is not to condone badly thought-out schemes, carbuncles which detract from an otherwise glorious landscape or ribbon development, but the signs are that those wanting to build good, high quality houses in very low densities will find themselves pushing on a door that is opening in the next few years, even if the rate of progress is slow.

AN HISTORICAL PRECEDENT

There is a good scene in *Headlong Hall*, by the nineteenth-century satirist

Thomas Love Peacock, in which Lord Littlebrain's picturesque improver, Mr Milestone, is showing off the plans for his lordship's country estate to the shapely Miss Tenorina. Mr Milestone proudly produces a sketch of a hilltop covered in trees and mossy rocks.

'What a delightful spot to read in, on a summer's day. The air must be so pure and the wind must sound so divinely in the tops of those old pines,' she says.

'Bad taste, Miss Tenorina. Bad taste, I assure you. Here is the spot improved. The trees are cut down: the stones are cleared away: this is an octagonal pavilion, exactly on the centre of the summit: and there you see Lord Littlebrain, on top of the pavilion enjoying the prospect with a telescope,' replies Milestone.

For much of the last century the little houses, prospect towers and follies which at one stage it was all the rage for the well-to-do to scatter around the countryside or plant on prime urban sites, were a bit of a joke, and a pretentious one at that, an attitude which partly explains the long years of neglect that many endured.

Today, they are prized, one-off monuments to that movement of the spirit in the eighteenth and nineteenth centuries which flowered in an appreciation of scenery, in the paintings of the English landscapists and the poems of Wordsworth. They are greatly sought after, and frequently converted into rather grand residences for new-age country lovers. Perhaps one day a new flowering of 1980s and 1990s individual homes will be seen in the same way, but Peacock did have a point, and the urge to over-improve needs to be kept strictly in check.

The easiest way of curbing one's own creative desires is either to buy one of the tested and proven packages available – or to hire a good architect.

In France, Germany or the United States young architects will cut their teeth by designing houses for private clients and managing the construction projects. In Britain, many architects go for the whole of their careers without ever seeing a house design of their own built.

In Scandinavia, companies offering ranges of package houses which can be bought in kit form and put up on a site of the purchaser's choosing make up a major portion of the market. In Britain they are a small, if expanding, part of the total.

Traditional self-build, where you do some of the banging together of the bits of wood and the moving of the piles of bricks, has been attracting a different audience in the UK as well, as it happens. By using timber-frame designs much of the drudgery is avoided, and some very good courses have been set up for those with little or no experience on a building site.

A decline in the overall number of projects could possibly mask a significant trend as publicly funded projects are overtaken by private schemes.

No longer are determined amateurs at the mercy of skilled professionals, who have all the experience and understanding of how a building site works. There are short courses which provide complete beginners with the basic skills and confidence to project manage plasterers, bricklayers and other subcontractors they may call in to do the complicated bits.

You probably need an aptitude for doing things with your hands, but experience of building is certainly not necessary, according to many of the organisers, and can be a positive disadvantage as you will have to unlearn bad habits before picking up the right ones.

Timber-frame construction techniques which rely on simple pad foundations can cut costs dramatically:

- By reducing expensive and time-consuming groundworks;
- Because the roof is designed to go up early, much of the work can go on under cover and the rest of the project is speeded up.

Self-build using this method can give savings of up to 50 per cent on the purchase price of an equivalent building, if all the labour costs as well as the contractor's profit are knocked out.

Horror stories abound about the messes people can find themselves pitched into by badly completed houses built by contractors. Perhaps putting the cement between the bricks yourself or watching while it is done are ways of making certain there is some there.

But most of us who want more say in the design and execution of our homes are either going to hire professionals in the form of architects or building subcontractors who know how to manage the project, or buy a package. These come as both timber-frame houses and as more traditional brick and block construction.

They are flexible and can now be found in styles varying from elaborate medieval hall houses complete with huge oak beams, through to pieces of high-tec design. In between are many popular designs which look remarkably like smart executive estate homes. The difference is that they can mostly be put together with internal configurations to achieve an individual customer's specification.

GREEN HOUSES AND ECOLOGY

Whatever route people choose to create a home of their own, the chances are that they will end up with more well-packaged modern technology, natural materials and energy-saving equipment than come with the conventional, off-the-peg builders' product.

It is not easy to make a pure economic case for much of this equipment, but perhaps people only get deeply involved in building projects if they are converts to the cause of green design, or at least sympathisers.

The problem for the volume builder is not hard to see. He is concerned, above all, with keeping costs down on most projects and if it is going to take, say, ten years to save, through lower fuel bills, the extra cost of a condensing boiler with heat exchange unit compared to the conventional gas gobbler, then hardly any builder will install one, no matter how often the Department of Energy lectures them that domestic buildings account for 62 per cent of energy use in the UK and that home heating produces 53 million tons of CO_2 in a year.

It is very unfair on the manufacturers of the energy-saving equipment, because heat exchangers and the like are not inherently much more expensive than ordinary boilers, but the economies of scale make the latter more competitive.

The only way to tip the balance is for the State to tax conventional boilers or increase the price of fuel to the point where they are shunned, and green equipment is no longer an oddity considered only by the deep green fringe. In reality, the technological changes of the past few years have opened up ecologically sound building in a way few would have predicted. There is now a huge array of new techniques and devices available and, if few of them are actually going to save much money in the short term, they all make houses safer, more pleasant and more comfortable places to live in.

Some really ought to be incorporated if you possibly can; the benefits are immediate. Good insulation is a must and, if designed from scratch, very easy to build in.

It is possible to get eminently practical systems which avoid the unpleasant chemicals of a vapour barrier and the associated condensation problems which plague many older properties. Insulation can be mostly made out of cellulose these days, which will breathe with the house.

Under-floor heating had an appalling reputation in the 1960s and 1970s because it cost so much to run. A friend of mine has an architect-designed penthouse (1970 vintage) on top of a London mansion block of 1890s vintage. It is a beautiful place – so long as you time your visit for good weather. If it is cold outside you freeze, because the electric floor heating elements cost something over £1 an hour to run. It was also built with minimal insulation so that any warmth, that by some fluke does get trapped, soon finds an escape route.

Today, under-floor heating systems employ flexible polystyrene pipes buried in the concrete pad and carrying warm water. They are insulated from below and heat the top of the pad, providing a more evenly heated environment than conventional radiators. You can even fit adaptations of the system into the voids between the joists of wooden floors (the pads sit in shallow pans which hang between the joists).

The result is that on the coldest winter day it is warm inside. No more sitting in front of the radiator, no more shivering in the cold kitchen; your house stays warm and, instead of heating the tops of rooms and the lamps hanging from the ceiling, the heat is where you want it, at floor level, with an even gradient getting cooler higher up.

Warmed air systems have also improved. When combined with a mechanical heat recovery system, which takes back the heat from the bathroom and kitchen exhausts to heat incoming fresh air, they produce warm and cosy rooms at a fraction of conventional heating costs.

The true enthusiast can even buy solar tubes which boost free energy collection and are designed to work in the diffused light of a grey English day.

Most new houses come with double glazing because, if planned from the inception of a project, it does not add hugely to the costs and will cut down on the draughts which make a room feel cold. For the serious insulator there are more advanced triple glazing systems available; these incorporate an argon barrier, which is such a bad conductor that virtually nothing gets through to the outside world. A big selection of glazing options are available. And you can build conservatories out of what is called low-energy glass, the idea being that they will stay warm virtually from the light of a 60 watt bulb on the coldest day.

Inside the house, levels of natural light are increased dramatically using the technology available for bigger and better windows and roof lights. Also, more thought goes into the design and placing of openings than was the case in the 1960s and 1970s.

Good quality joinery and furniture in temperate hardwoods are no longer expensive, although there has been some debate about the green credentials of temperate hardwoods, which some argue are in the same danger as tropical varieties.

But you can get sisal and coir floor coverings which both look elegant and are far cheaper than many conventional floor coverings. Like plant-based paint finishes they breathe and are not toxic.

In short, with thought and imagination you can create an environment which is markedly more civilised than that of most conventional new homes, and which spends the available budget sensibly.

BREAKING THE MOULD

Sadly, imagination is a commodity in very short supply on the British domestic architectural scene. UK volume housing hardly inspires.

One cause is the deep disenchantment with the mess that town planners made of so many town centres and civic buildings during the 1960s. Town councils across the country found themselves taking delivery of inferior buildings and the inhabitants quite rightly did not like the results.

Another is the sneaking feeling – reinforced by some estate agents – that anything 'arty' or unusual will be difficult to sell. Taken to its logical conclusion this desire to find and stick with whatever the mass market finds least fault with would have had us all living in pastiche neo-Georgian houses.

But market-dictated greyness is on the wain because much of the short-termism of the housing market has now gone. If you are going to spend the best part of a decade in a home you might as well spend the money on one you really want.

Decent design is sadly not always the top priority for some self-builders, partly, one suspects, because they are short of cash and one of the first casualties is the aesthetics of the thing. Faced with a choice between extra kitchen cupboards plus a large utility room or an elegant, well-designed façade, many have gone for the cupboards.

Inspiring new British designs

Although most British architects do not grow fat on domestic commissions, there has been a consistent flow of breathtakingly good designs which have been built in the last few years, and although these houses cover the broadest possible spectrum – from gleaming high tec using the techniques and materials of prefabricated commercial construction, through to delicate and exquisitely detailed essays in Classicism – the best are packed with all the comforts and technology of the late twentieth century fitted into spaces tailored to late twentieth-century patterns of living.

Richard Horden's Boat House at Poole in Dorset was completed in the early 1980s, but it is still one of the most interesting examples of the use of industrial components and techniques, drawing on both the Modernist tradition and the best of the quick fabrication methods developed in the last few years.

The designer is a keen yachtsman, something reflected in the extensive use of standard yacht components. Steel cables are anchored to upright steel posts by shackles and sail cloth which, when pulled taut over window openings, provides optional shade in some areas. Along with steel, aluminium and plastics are also put to extensive use, creating a giant modular box based on a grid plan.

Architects like Ian Ritchie have developed the same sort of neo-industrial concepts although, by using standard components rather than hand-crafted one-offs, the cost can be cut dramatically.

Ritchie's Eagle Rock House near Uckfield in Sussex was built out of steel frames to form a cross with a raised atrium in a central living space where the two basic elements meet. It was built for a keen horticulturist with the living areas leading to a raised rear section. Two wings, set at an angle to the atrium, are filled with bedrooms, bathrooms and the working parts of the building. The steel siding has been covered with trellis at the points where there are no window openings, the idea being that as the vegetation grows it will partially camouflage the structure.

You can take advantage of the economies of scale in the mass production of the basic elements of a house like this, and end up with a building that is imaginative yet carefully fitted to any special requirements you wish to incorporate, without it costing a fortune.

Classical reality

In some ways it seems light years from these minimalist creations in steel and glass to a house like Ashfold House, also in Sussex.

This is a deliberate, careful and complex piece of classicism, but beautifully presented as a compact modern residence (it is about 2500 square feet in area) and filled with a deceptively large amount of modern technology.

It was designed by John Simpson as a home for his parents. (The 'house for mother' syndrome, it should be said, is a traditional route to getting something built for many architects, including the academic giants of modernism, who for so long dominated the American and British architectural establishments.) Simpson is best known for his heroic scheme for Paternoster Square by St Paul's Cathedral. In October 1992, as a virtual unknown, he pulled off a coup and defeated the modernists when his scheme for the redevelopment of the square around St Paul's, employing a traditional street plan and low-rise buildings designed in accordance with classical principles, was given the go-ahead.

With the country house he was heavily influenced by Sir John Soane, the architectural genius whose master work, the old Bank of England, was demolished in the 1920s in one of the great acts of cultural vandalism of the century.

The plan at Ashfold is loosely based on Soane's own country house, Pitzhanger Manor in Ealing, although it is smaller, more regular and has a central hall rising the full height of the building. Soane set his hall to one side, but by using a sophisticated central heating system Simpson was released from the constraint of keeping the limited warmth under tight control and did not have to box his staircase or create buffer areas against draughts.

An ingenious system of folding window shutters has been used in preference to double glazing, which tends to require thicker glazing bars in order to support the extra weight.

Other technology is incorporated in a disguised form. The infrared sensors of the security system have been incorporated into candle holders set into the walls, and cabinets designed by the architect in the living room on either side of the elaborate, curling fireplace open to reveal televisions, video equipment and the panoply of modern electronic entertainment.

That is hardly a novel trick, but the point is that at Ashfold the whole building is so correctly in proportion. It looks a far larger house than it actually is, and sits in harmony with its landscape, the kitchen garden of an earlier house, and its strong historical references make sense in the context.

There was, in fact, a minor rash of new country villas built in the late 1980s on the crest of the Thatcher boom, with architects like John Outram managing to create something of a mini-vogue, and a base of rich clients who both had taste and wanted to commission something was slowly beginning to emerge.

The depth and length of the recession knocked that particular trend back a bit, and it seems unlikely that the opulent interiors of Outram's expanded classicism will be widely copied, but there is a rich pool of source material and well-executed pioneering works in a kaleidoscope of different styles around.

A house looking like a Japanese-style pagoda, made of glass and set in central Scotland, sounds like a recipe for very uncomfortable and cold nights. Young architects Andrew Whalley and Fiona Galbraith, however, designed a retirement house based loosely on a Japanese pagoda for Whalley's parents in the village of Dollar, central Scotland, and it is an outstanding success, winning a prestigious award in 1992.

The bungalow is in the shape of a square doughnut, with a glass-roofed winter garden in the central courtyard. Rooms on all four sides open from this green space and the brief was to produce the finished house for under £65,000, excluding the kitchen.

Two of the outside walls are made of glass and the roof has an oriental awning, in the style of a pagoda. The other two walls are solid stone and back on to the road.

Rather than setting the house as far back from the road as possible, as most conventional designs tend to do, here the building backs right on to the road with the two blind stone walls up against the roadside boundary.

The three bedrooms and two bathrooms are at the back, with illumination from roof lights – an arrangement which works well because during the day most time tends to be spent in either the courtyard or the main living rooms. The living room, dining room and kitchen look out through glass walls to an outside walled garden which is both private and shielded from some of the prevailing winds.

Extra light comes in via high-level mirrors set above the low-energy glass. During the summer, no heating is needed, and bills are far lower than for a conventional house for the rest of the year. If the meter reader can't get in, estimated fuel bills are always pleasingly ahead of the amount they actually use.

The elderly couple said they wanted a single storey house with bedrooms and conservatory on the same level. Whalley decided that the corridor you usually find in a bungalow was a waste of space, hence the winter garden.

The only drawback according to his mother, Marjorie Whalley, is that Japanese inspired design works best with a minimalist approach to decoration, but she has still put up some curtains, even if it detracts from the bare aesthetics.

I am not sure I particularly like the end result; it reminds me a little of municipal school architecture of the 1960s from the façade with the glass sides, and I'm not sure that minimalism really goes very well in a retirement house for a couple living in Scotland. However, the idea of having a central atrium accessed from many rooms of a single-storey building is very clever, and the building is bright in the areas where light is important and darker in those where it is not.

Architect Chris Cowper achieved a startling, if in many ways traditional, result in a commission to turn a wooden barracks into a house in the fenland village of Cottenham. He added a tower complete with terrace to one end, producing a compact six-bedroom house in the process, which is covered in brightly painted blue and yellow ochre clapboard.

Here the owners set a budget limit of £100,000 to pay for everything, and the end result is the kind of interesting wooden-clad house which ought to be far more popular than it has been in recent years in Britain. Here, there is still a fixation with brick and stone claddings, despite the fact that across much of North America and northern Europe wooden-clad buildings are the preferred choice for far more extreme climates than those of the British Isles.

TAKING THE PLUNGE

The obstacles to building the house of your dreams are eroding, and once you set out on the self-build road there is a lot of good advice to be had, if you know where to find it. This book outlines the main issues involved in getting a project off the ground. It is hoped that it will be of use to all individual home-builders, from those who are inspired to commission an architect to manage a whole project, through to those who buy modest packages and set about putting in some of the slog themselves, as well as the intrepid few who decide to do it all themselves.

2023 sq. ft. 4 Bedroomed Chalet

CHAPTER 2

THAT SPECIAL HOUSE

TOM ROWLAND

Choosing a design is one of the most enjoyable parts of planning an individual home. However, glancing through the large number of existing house plans available in magazines, books and company brochures is sometimes a daunting and confusing experience that can lead you round in circles. The problem is in finding a design that measures up to a long list of your requirements – budget, style, layout, site conditions, taste; the list goes on. However, following a few basic ground rules can make the process far easier.

One solution is to look at the key elements of a design independently, ideally by first selecting the house type – bungalow, dormer bungalow, etc, then by looking at the floor plan, and lastly by looking at the external style and appearance.

No book can be comprehensive enough to contain every conceivable floor plan arrangement, for every single house type and then illustrate it in every single style. In many instances, the location of the proposed house may limit the choice of house type open to the self-builder. For example, the location may dictate that the external appearance must be in the vernacular, or that the house is single-storey.

The rule to remember is that if you like something about one design, whether it is just the floor plan, the style of the exterior, or even just one feature, it is usually possible to incorporate it within your chosen design, although the result might look horrible. Existing floor plans can be altered without changing the external appearance of a design. Equally, the external appearance of a design can be altered to suit any area, without having to alter the floor plan.

An example of how both design and materials can be altered to suit different requirements is the Avonmere design, created by package supplier, Design and Materials Ltd. A successful design for the company for the past 12 years or so, the original Avonmere was a Tudor-style house with a floor area of over 3000 square feet, requiring a good-sized plot.

Many of the company's clients liked the design, but wanted a smaller or larger version or were worried that the Tudor style would be at odds with their local planning policies. This gave rise to the creation of many new designs which, although different in their own small way, still retain the traditional character of the original design.

Illustrated here are two examples of variations on the original Avonmere design, each of them redrawn in three different regional styles.

VARIATIONS ON THE SAME FLOOR PLAN

Stock bricks with render and Tudor boarding to first floor. Casement windows with Jacobean leaded glass. Double Roman roof tiles with square bargeboards.

Natural stone with traditional window surrounds, label moulds and gable vents. Casement windows with diamond leaded glass. Slate roof with stone tabled verges.

Facing brick with herringbone brick panels and Tudor boarding to first floor. Casement windows with Jacobean leaded glass. Plain clay tiles to roof with hung tiles to porch.

Facing bricks with brick detailing and plinth. Cottage bar casement windows. Plain clay roof tiles with feature bullnose courses, fleur-de-lis ridges and scalloped bargeboards.

Stock bricks with render and Tudor boarding to first floor. Casement windows with Jacobean leaded glass. Pantiled roof with square bargeboards.

Natural stone with quoins and render to first floor. Traditional sash and case windows. Natural slate roof with pointed verges.

ARCHITECTURAL DETAILING

A new house does not have to look new, and given enough time and a generous budget the most unpromising of cement block barracks can be decorated with elements from an earlier building style. The judicious placing of genuine architectural elements can, if done properly, add a stylish touch.

But extreme caution is required, and more often than not the result is a garish pudding where the elements scream at each other and the owners – did they but know it – have turned themselves into laughing stocks. Cherry picking requires skill.

It also pays to make proper enquiries as to the provenance of items. It is illegal to remove fittings or fixtures from listed buildings, an increasingly common source for a great many objects, although it should be added that many of the pieces on the market have been obtained quite legitimately by reputable dealers. However, it pays to check rather than assume.

Architectural antiques have become a popular target for thieves, and buyers of possibly stolen goods could help to stem the illegal trade. The theft of houses' finest fittings flourishes during a recession. There are more people out of work looking for easy money, more families are staying put because they cannot sell their houses and are instead doing them up, and in cities, old office buildings stay empty longer, presenting an easy target for casual larceny.

The theft of those bits of someone else's house that people buy to enhance their own has become an epidemic, according to conservationists, and it is not just the most valuable artifacts of obvious beauty and value that disappear. Victorian houses that are empty and for sale lose light switches, door handles, stained glass and internal doors. York paving stones disappear from pavements.

Even when old pieces of other buildings have a perfectly respectable background, have been thoughtfully incorporated, and the desired effect comes off, there is always the lingering feeling that the ancient doors, Adam-style marble fireplaces or Victorian cupolas would have looked a great deal better in their original locations.

But it would not do to be too much of a killjoy; after all, not everything is bent or botched. Perhaps the most extreme example of what can be done by a dedicated architectural salvage magpie is the slightly ridiculous but amusing West Ley, near South Molton in Devon.

This is a completely modern house, made out of breeze block within the last few years, but it has been crammed with an enormous number of architectural antiques by the dealer owners, who used it as a showcase for their business before putting it on the market.

Much of the façade of the long, low house under a steeply pitched slate roof is certainly old, but hardly in its original place. The leaded light windows sporting oak mullions came from a Welsh manor house, the doors from a French chateau, and the elaborately carved bargeboards on either side of the porch from heaven knows where.

Inside, there is a fifteenth-century oak staircase. The ceiling timbers come from a Normandy barn, the bathroom tiles from a long-demolished trade union building in London and the spiral staircase linking the living room to an upstairs bedroom is from a Second World War bomber airfield control tower; one washbasin is from an old French railway carriage.

Some parts work well; in the kitchen a cobalt blue Aga is set off by a carved, pink marble sink and drainer with antique Portuguese tiles, but a vaulted dining room, with its exposed ceiling trusses and wall decorations believed to be from a seventeenth-century convent in Barnstaple, hardly suits a modest little house.

Not surprisingly, this confection has had a lot of press coverage – it even featured in a television documentary – and if it is over the top, it is still worth remembering as an antidote to the grinding earnestness that seems to dog many individual home projects. A little wit and a lightness of touch never did any harm.

SELF-BUILD AND AUCTIONS

Be it bits to incorporate into the structure of your house or pieces to set off the structure once it is built, it is worth getting into the auction habit when you embark on a building project. During the recession of the early 1990s, an unprecedented mountain of hardware, property and artworks belonging to the repossessed and the dispossessed has cascaded on to the auction market, and those prepared to spend a little time can pick up real bargains.

On the Continent, 80 per cent of the bidders at auctions are members of the public and only 20 per cent are dealers; here the reverse is true. Although the auction business is still one of the UK's success industries, leading the world table in turnover, and London is second only to New York as the art market capital, buying at auction is still a minority activity.

Large quantities of builders' materials are also sold at auction each year: it is not just antiques and old window frames that come under the hammer. Regular liquidation sales are held in London's East End and commercial centres around the country, sadly more than ever during the economic downturn.

The trick is finding out about them; even the auction houses can be remarkably reticent about publicising events, and a surprising number regard members of the public, who might not pay on time and clog up an otherwise smooth operation, as unpredictable nuisances.

You can see their point: if the object of the day is to sell the machinery in an engineering plant, someone who is only there to pick up an odd lot of scaffold bars which are certain to go for next to nothing *is* a nuisance. But for those on the look out for cheap scaffolding, it is worth persisting.

There are now a number of publications which can help to track down the more obscure no reserve and liquidation sales: *The Government Auction Handbook* (£12.95) and the *Government Auction News* (annual subscription only; £39.50 first year), 3rd Floor, Bastille Court, 2 Paris Garden, London SE1 8ND (Tel: 071–928 6956); *Saleroom and Auction Monthly*, Applegate Publishing, PO Box 107, Guildford, Surrey GU1 1EB.

Spring and autumn sales of architectural antiques are also regularly staged around the country. Christie's runs sales at Wrotham Park in Hertfordshire, where the lots have a bias towards items for interiors, while Sotheby's has sales concentrating more on garden statuary and decorative objects at Billingshurst.

One of the largest selections of purely architectural sundries – columns, pediments, obelisks, railings and old stone – is to be found in the regular auctions by Posterity, held at Norton, near Gloucester GL2 9LN (Tel: 0452 731850).

Brillscote Farm, Lea, near Malmesbury in Wiltshire specialises in auctioning architectural and decorative items including garden antiques, and has a range of oddities from pairs of carved wooden pillars to the interior of a nineteenth-century grocer's shop, including the counter, coffee grinder and display cabinets. Details may be obtained from the London representatives, Relic Antiques (Tel: 071–387 6039 or 071–359 2597. Relic Antiques also have an outlet at 21 Camden Passage, London N1.

ARCHITECTS, MANAGEMENT AND TRAINING FOR SELF-BUILD

Association of Self-Builders
Hollow End, Hollow Lane, Colton, Rugeley, Staffs WS15 3LQ
Tel: 0889 584221
Self-help and sound advice.

Brick Development Association Ltd
Woodside House, Winkfield, Windsor, Berks SL4 2DX
Tel: 0344 885651

Building Centre
26 Store Street, London WC1E 7BT
Tel: 071–637 1022
Information about building materials.

Community Self-Build Agency, The
Unit 26, Finsbury Business Centre,
40 Bowling Green Lane, London EC1R 0NE
Tel: 071–415 7092

Constructive Individuals
47A Brushfield Street, Spitalfields Market, London E1 6AA
Tel: 071–377 6763
Downing Villa, 36 Scarcroft Road, York YO2 1NF
Tel: 0904 625300
Architects. DIY and self-build training courses.

Individual House Builders Association
(IHBA is a trade association which also takes individual members)
107 Lancaster Gate, London W2 3NQ
Tel: 071–262 2218

Juvan Courses
Lower House, Mill Lane, Longhope, Glos GL17 0AA
Tel: 0452 831348
DIY and self-build training courses.

National Federation of Housing Associations
North West Regional Office, Warwickgate House, Warwick Road,
Manchester M16 0DD (Contact Roland Ashley.)
Tel: 061–848 8132

Royal Institute of British Architects, The (RIBA)
66 Portland Place, London W1N 4AD
Tel: 071–580 5533
Good advice line and help in finding the right architect.

Skillbuilding
Letitia Street, Middlesbrough, Cleveland TS5 4BE
Tel: 0642 221314
Promotes training and user involvement in public house building.

Walter Segal Self-Build Trust, The
PO Box 542, London SE1 1TX
Tel: 071–833 4152

NB: *Manufacturers are a good source of technical information.*

ORGANISATIONS INTERESTED IN GREEN BUILDING

Association of Environment Conscious Building, The
Windlake House, The Pump Field, Coaley, Glos GL11 5DX
Tel: 0453 890757

Bristol Energy Centre
101 Philip Street, Bedminster, Bristol, Avon BS3 4DR
Tel: 0272 662008
Advice centre.

Building Research Establishment
Bucknalls Lane, Garston, Watford, Herts WD2 7JR
Tel: 0923 894040

Centre for Alternative Technology
Machynlleth, Powys, Wales SY20 9AZ
Tel: 0654 702400
Excellent bookshop, visitors centre and display.

Ecological Design Association, The
20 High Street, Stroud, Glos GL5 1AS
Tel: 0453 765575

Energy Advisory Services
The Old Manor House, Hanslope,
Milton Keynes MK19 7LS
Tel: 0908 510596

Energy Efficiency Office
Department of the Environment, 1 Palace Street,
London SW1E 5HE
Tel: 071–238 3105

Energy Technology Support Unit (ETSU)
Harwell, Didcot, Oxon OX11 0RA
Tel: 0235 821000

Institute of Building Biology, The
c/o White Horse House, Crown Hill, Ashdon, Saffron Walden,
Essex CB10 2ET

MVM Starpoint
Home Energy Labels Department, 16 Park Place, Clifton,
Bristol BS8 1JP
Tel: 0272 253769

National Energy Foundation
Rockingham Drive, Linford Wood, Milton Keynes MK14 6EG
Tel: 0908 672787

Timber Research & Development Association
Stocking Lane, Hughenden Valley, High Wycombe, Bucks HP1A 4ND
Tel: 0494 563091

PACKAGE HOUSE SUPPLIERS

Berg Hus (Europe) Ltd
Bilton Mill Road, West Chiltington, Pulborough,
West Sussex RH20 2PY
Tel: 0798 812896

Custom Homes Ltd
45 Station Road, Redhill, Surrey RH1 1QH
Tel: 0737 768261

Design and Materials Ltd
Lawn Road, Carlton in Lindrick Industrial Estate, Worksop,
Notts S81 9LB
Tel: 0909 730333

Hedlunds Swedish Houses Ltd
Hedlunds House, Beacon Road, Crowborough, East Sussex TN6 1AF
Tel: 0892 665007

Hosby Sale Ltd
Unit 24, The Nursery, High Street, Sutton Courtenay, Nr Abingdon,
Oxon OX14 4UA
Tel: 0235 848756

Lindal Cedar Homes
PO Box 3, Bottesford, Notts NG13 0EZ
Tel: 0949 42551

Medina Gimson Ltd
Bordyke End, East Street, Tonbridge, Kent TN9 1HA
Tel: 0732 770992

Myresjo UK Ltd
5 Hyde Park Gate, London SW7 5EW
Tel: 071–584 8737

Nordic Homes Ltd
Majority House, 51 Lodge Lane, Derby DE1 3HB
Tel: 0332 203040

Oliver Homes
Burnfoot Industrial Estate, Hawick, Scotland TD9 8SL
Tel: 0450 73283

Potton Ltd
The Old Foundry, Willow Road, Potton, Nr Sandy, Beds SG19 2PP
Tel: 0767 260348

Prestoplan Homes Ltd
Four Oaks Road, Walton Summit, Preston, Lancs PR5 8AS
Tel: 0772 627373

Scandia-Hus Ltd
Crown Lodge, Cantelupe Road, East Grinstead, West Sussex
RH19 3YU
Tel: 0342 327977

MEB Home Improvements are showing their commitment to energy conservation by supplying the finest and most advanced solar water heating system on the market today. MEB's guarantee and standards of service stand behind these cost effective, high performance, vacuum tube Hitachi/NEG solar systems.

Residential, commercial users, and swimming pool owners have discovered the environmentally safe way to save substantially on their annual fuel bills and have found that solar is the only method of heating which increases savings the more it is used.

Swimming pool heating is particularly suited for Solar Energy use. By circulating a large volume of water through the system at relatively low temperatures, advantage can be taken of the greater efficiency in heat collection. MEB Home Improvements can extend the swimming comfort zone and your swimming season by installing an energy saving MEB solar pool system to any size of pool.

The MEB's Solar system will really make a difference to your lifestyle. In addition to reducing your energy bills and the impact of future cost increases, the system will increase the value of your home. You will help to conserve our finite fossil fuel resources and protect our natural environment.

At the heart of every MEB Solar Water heating system is a dual sensor electronic controller, which constantly monitors the availability of solar energy. The installed system is fully automatic in operation and requires minimal maintenance. Over temperature, over pressure and frost protection are provided as standard.

MEB's flexible Home Improvement Loans with optional credit protection insurance are available from £1000 – £15000 to take care of your solar purchase needs. For more information call us now Free on 0800-400428. A solar energy consultant will be pleased to come and discuss your requirements.

Solar So Good

The most efficient way of heating your water is with solar energy. But how do you go about it? Well MEB can install solar panels to your roof and connect them to your existing hot water system with the minimum of fuss.

One panel will catch and convert enough energy to heat your water throughout the spring, summer and autumn months. Even in winter, the sun emits enough energy to significantly heat the water in your tank.

Swimmers won't be left out in the cold either, because solar panels can convert enough energy to heat a swimming pool for weeks on end.

Best of all, solar power is one of the few truly 'green' sources of energy. So not only will you be saving money on fuel bills - you'll be helping the environment as well.

For more information call: **0800 400 428** or clip the coupon below, for a free brochure.

HELPING THE EARTH
BEGINS AT HOME

MEB Home Improvements, FREEPOST, Mucklow Hill, Halesowen, West Midlands. B62 8BP

I would like to know more about **Solar** water heating.

Name

Daytime Tel. No.   Evening Tel No.

Address

Postcode

MEB
home
IMPROVEMENTS

Who else would you trust in your home?

Another service from MEB (Contracting) Ltd, a subsidiary of Midlands Electricity plc.   DTIH6.94

FURTHER READING

Building Your Future: Self-Build Initiatives for the Unemployed and *Self-Build: A Manual for Self-Build Housing Associations*, 1988, National Federation of Housing Associations

Building Your Own Home, Murray Armor, 1976, revised 1993, Vent Press

Buildings and Health, The Rosehaugh Guide to the Design, Construction, Use and Management of Buildings, 1990, RIBA Publications

The Build It Guide to Managing The Building of Your Own Timber Frame Home, Rosalind Renshaw, 1993, Build It Publications

Co-housing, Kathryn McCamant and Charles Durrett, 1988, Habitat Press

Design for the Real World, Victor Papanek, 1985, 2nd edition, Thames and Hudson

Eco-Renovation, Edward Harland, 1993, Green Books

Energy Efficiency in Domestic Electrical Appliances, (Energy Efficiency Office), 1990, Energy Technology Support Unit, HMSO

Energy Efficient Housing: A Timber Framed Approach, Geoffrey Pitts, 1989, Timber Research and Development Association

The Good Wood Guide, Friends of the Earth, 1988

Green Architecture: Design for a Sustainable Future, Brenda and Robert Vale, 1991, Thames and Hudson

Green Design, A Guide to the Environmental Impact of Building Materials, Avril Fox and Robin Murrell, 1989, Architecture, Design and Technology Press

Green Engineering, A Current Awareness Bulletin, E Ellis, Institute of Mechanical Engineering

Guide to Green Buildings, London Ecology Unit

Hazardous Building Materials, A Guide to the Selection of Alternatives, S R Curwell and C G March, 1986, E & F N Spon

Healthy Buildings, Bill Holdsworth and Anthony Sealey, 1991, Architecture, Design and Technology Press; 1992, Longman

Healthy Housing, A Practical Guide, Ray Ranson, 1991, E and F N Spon

The Independent Home, Michael Potts, 1993, Green Books

Issues in Design: Green Design, David Burrell, 1991, The Design Council

The Natural House Book, David Pearson, 1989, Conran Octopus

Places of Soul: Architecture & Environmental Design as a Healing Art, Christopher Day, 1993, Aquarian Press

Practical Housebuilding, Robert Matthews, 1991, Blackberry Books

The Self-Build Book, Jon Broome/Brian Richardson, 1991, Green Books

Sick Building Syndrome, London Hazards Centre, 1990

Simple Build Green, John Talbot, 1993, Findhorn Foundation

The Solar Electric House, Steven Strong, 1993, Green Books

Talking About Self-Build, Robert Matthews, 1990, Blackberry Books

Towards a Green Architecture, Brenda and Robert Vale, 1991, RIBA Publications

Use of CFCs in Building, S R Curwell, R C Fox and C G March, 1988, Fernsheer

CHAPTER 3

FINANCING AN INDIVIDUAL HOME

MICHAEL ERGATOUDIS

Michael Ergatoudis is the Editor of *Individual Homes* magazine and writes regularly on personal finance for a number of national magazines.

RAISING FINANCE

Loan finance for all forms of property acquisition has changed considerably since the liberal days of the late 1980s, when house price inflation appeared to be in an eternally upward spiral and lenders virtually fell over one another to extend credit. When property prices finally hit the ceiling in 1989 and then began their rapid descent, banks and building societies alike began to tighten up their lending policies in an attempt to minimise their losses. Not least hit by this general credit squeeze has been finance for individual home-build.

Although the majority of the major high street lenders are still prepared to offer up to 100 per cent of building costs to those wishing to build their own home, none is now prepared to loan 100 per cent of the cost of a plot of building land. With no security for finance other than the value of the plot itself, the maximum any lender is prepared to advance for land is

90 per cent of its open market value. This constraint on lending has made individual home-build less accessible for many households. Those who previously relied on 100 per cent finance must now raise a deposit of at the very least 15 per cent of the total project cost in order to get started.

Despite this precondition, 18,000 or more households succeeded in building their own home in 1992, the majority of them using loan finance.

Land purchase and building costs are usually financed using independent loans that work in quite different ways. Only when the project is complete will they both be paid off by an ordinary mortgage, secured against the new property.

Of course, not everyone requires finance for both land and build. For those lucky enough to own a building plot already, raising the finance to build a home on it is still relatively straightforward. Provided there is sufficient income to service the repayments, most lenders, including the major high street banks, will be prepared to consider offering building finance.

Under these circumstances, most lenders will offer up to a maximum of 100 per cent of the cost of the project, provided it does not exceed 90 to 95 per cent of the overall value of the finished building.

This is assessed in advance by the lender's valuers who will look at the project plans and assess how much the property to be constructed will be worth when completed. There is a fee for this and it will usually be around £120–£150, rising in proportion to the amount of work involved. As a well-planned and well-executed project will usually be valued at between 15 to 40 per cent more than it has cost to build, the maximum lending constraint of 95 per cent is not usually the factor that limits borrowing.

The usual limitation on the size of the loan is based on what the lender believes the customer can reasonably afford to repay. This is calculated by using income multipliers of three times the higher income, plus one times the lower income, or, alternatively, 2.5 times the sum of the joint incomes. However, these maximum multiples can vary between lenders.

Loans for building work are usually released in stages, in arrears. For a detached house, there are most commonly four stages, each of 25 per cent of the total build cost. Under such a scheme, stage payments will be released on completion of the 'first floor', 'roofed', 'plastered and fitted' and 'completed'.

With some lenders, these stages can be adjusted to suit individual circumstances. They will also vary for bungalows or other types of property. Some lenders offer special schemes for customers building using timber-frame construction.

Until the release of each stage payment, the individual home-builder must finance all the building work independently. If there is sufficient equity held in the plot (well over 25 per cent), funds for the building work could possibly be borrowed against this. A precondition of this is that there is sufficient income to cover the additional repayments. Alternatively, the funds to complete building work in between the stages can be found through other sources, such as bank overdrafts, building accounts and credit with suppliers. For most projects, it will be necessary to have a total of at least 20–25 per cent of the total build cost (excluding land) available in cash and credit to provide a cash flow between stage payments.

Underestimating cash flow requirement is one of the most common mistakes made in the organisation of private home-build projects. To overcome this, it is a good idea to develop a cash flow forecast. This matter is dealt with in the budgeting section of this chapter (pages 50–51).

Before funds are released, following the completion of each stage of the building work, the lender will arrange for its surveyor to inspect the property and re-value it. Provided the work is of a satisfactory standard, funds will be released. A fee of between £30 to £50 is charged for each re-inspection. On completion of the last stage of the project, the outstanding balance of the loan is paid off by a mortgage taken out on the new property and repaid in the normal way.

The majority of individual home-builders are not lucky enough to own a plot already and require an advance for at least a proportion of the cost of buying one. In late 1993, brokers reported that around 60 lenders were offering finance for both land and build, including most of the major building societies and the major clearing banks. In addition to up to 100 per cent of build costs, the various finance schemes offer different proportions of the cost of a building plot, ranging from 25 per cent up to a maximum of 90 per cent.

For all but a few households (those with large savings), the maximum loan of 90 per cent of the value of a plot usually means first having to sell any existing home that has an outstanding mortgage on it.

Many lenders have made the sale of any existing home with an outstanding mortgage a mandatory precondition for their customers, leaving them no option but to move into temporary accommodation during the build. This need not be as bad as it sounds. In most cases it means renting a home conveniently near to the site. Alternatively, it can mean buying a mobile home or caravan and living on the site. In some cases, it is possible to move in with friends or relations for a few months until the new house is complete.

In some circumstances, it may be possible to avoid selling the existing home, by borrowing the additional funds required towards the cost of a plot. Lenders are not keen to do this and will try to discourage it, regardless of the household's income or the security they have to offer. However, in theory at least, provided there are sufficient assets against which to secure the additional borrowing, lenders will consider capital raising loans, remortgages and bridging finance. They may also consider lending against other assets such as stocks and shares, a pension or life policy or any other redeemable savings policy or asset.

Additional lending for land acquisition most commonly takes the form of bridging finance. This is short-term lending, made using the equity in one property to buy another, usually pending an imminent sale. All such borrowing is likely to be at a premium rate, compared to the interest charged on land and build finance. As with all loans, any additional borrowing will be subject to lenders' usual criteria and proof of income.

Once the deposit for the land has been raised, the remaining funds for the purchase will be advanced. Finance for the build will then progress as it does for those who already own a plot. Funds to complete building work up until the release of the first stage payment must be available. This will usually be a combination of savings, overdraft, building society accounts and credit from suppliers. However, if there is sufficient equity in the plot (well over 25 per cent), funds towards the build may be borrowed, provided there is sufficient income to guarantee the additional repayments. Stage payments will then be released on the satisfactory completion of each stage of the building work, as described for those who already own their plot.

On completion of the project, the total of the outstanding loans for

WHEN YOUR HOUSE IS AT THIS LEVEL YOUR MORTGAGE PAYMENTS SHOULD BE TOO.

You've found your site, you've had the plans drawn, you've marked out the ground.

Now's the moment when your dream home could become a nightmare.

How on Earth do you find a mortgage? You go to Bradford & Bingley.

We'll give you a Progress Mortgage. It'll pay for your home, and even for the land.

But in stages. So that at any one time you'll only be paying interest on the work so far.

Apart from saving yourself plenty of money, this system helps you think out

your building project stage by stage, so your head can rule your heart.

So if you're thinking of putting together a dream home there's one building you ought to look into. Your nearest Bradford & Bingley.

For full details of Bradford & Bingley mortgages, write to FREEPOST, Bradford & Bingley Building Society, Bingley, West Yorkshire BD16 2LW, or phone free on 0800 252 993. (DTPM)

BRADFORD & BINGLEY
BUILDING SOCIETY

BUILDING YOUR OWN HOME?

Try a Progress Mortgage from Bradford & Bingley

Finance is one aspect of the self build process which people frequently report finding the most daunting part of the whole process. The idea of borrowing a large amount of money against a level site may seem incomprehensible however, Bradford & Bingley can help with the aid of a Progress Mortgage.

Many people, on contacting their existing lender, find that their bank or building society is only willing to offer them a loan once the property has reached a particular stage which can leave the borrower with the problem of financing the work up to that particular point. Others find that the organisation has to make special arrangements in order to accommodate their needs and this can potentially lead to problems with what is a non-standard system. However, Bradford & Bingley has developed a special mortgage especially for people who wish to have a property built to their own design. The Progress Mortgage is available through all of the Society's branches and stands alongside other offers which have been developed in order to meet the particular needs of our borrowers. All of the terms and conditions of the mortgage are clearly laid out from the start.

The Progress Mortgage has been designed to ensure that your payments are at their lowest at a time when your house is incomplete. Payments rise only as and when additional money is requested in order to fund the cost of the construction work, or when there is a rise in interest rates.

Under the terms of the Progress Mortgage up to 75% of the VALUE of the land (with detailed planning permission) can be obtained initially. From this point onwards, the Society will advance up to a maximum of 75% of the VALUE of the property as building work proceeds.

There are five standard stages at which Bradford & Bingley suggest that it may be appropriate for customers to request additional money for their building work. These stages are as follows:

(**1**) To purchase (or re-finance the purchase of) the building plot.

(**2**) When the property has reached ground floor sill level.

(**3**) When the property is wind and water tight ie. roofed in, brickwork completed, window frames and doors in place.

(**4**) Completion of plastering, installation and connection of all the services ie. gas, electric, water and telephone.

(**5**) Completion of the building fit for habitation, paths and drives and fencing in place.

Where the construction method is based around a timber frame rather than traditional bricks and mortar the suggested second stage release is once the timber shell has been constructed.

Bradford & Bingley aims to be as flexible as possible in relation to the release of funds in order to take into account the individual requirements and needs of such individual projects. Should customers find they are in a position where they have substantial bills to meet at a particular point in time, a visit by one of the Society's valuers can be requested. Then, subject to a satisfactory report, additional money can be released.

Planning permission for the building work should ideally be less than 2 years old at the time of application. Cases which fall outside this criteria are not automatically rejected but are subject to more stringent evaluation. The detailed plans for the proposed project are an important part of the mortgage application because they provide the society with a guide as to the final value of the property. This has an impact on the amount of money which can be released at different stages of construction.

The Society requires the building work to be carried out by contractors who are employed to handle the work. In order to ensure that the work meets recognised standards the construction must be covered by Custom Build (or New Build) or the builder be registered with NHBC. Alternatively the building process should be supervised by a qualified architect and an architects certificate should be produced every time additional advances are required.

Bradford & Bingley requires buildings insurance to be in place from the outset inorder to cover the project incase the worst should happen. In addition, the society also requires the site to be fully insured.

Building a property of your own can represent significant savings on buying a property which is already standing because self-builders do not have many of the over-heads which developers have to meet eg. office over-heads, staffing costs, sales costs and corporation tax.

The Progress Mortgage represents a cost effective way of financing a building project. The money is drawn down when it is needed and interest is only paid on the amount loaned at any one time. The rate of interest charged is base rate throughout the project. Details of the Society's current rate can be obtained by contacting any of the Society's branches.

The Society recognises that the self-build schemes are, by their very nature, individual and therefore the Progress Mortgage is designed to be as flexible as possible to meet those needs. By initially lending money for the purchase of the land itself (or to allow for re-financing if you already own the plot), money is released which can fund the traditionally expensive early stages of your project – a fact which is especially useful for timber-framed construction projects.

If you are considering having your own new home designed and built to your specifications but are concerned about how to finance the project, contact your local Bradford & Bingley branch to discuss your needs in detail.

WHEN YOUR HOUSE IS AT THIS LEVEL YOUR MORTGAGE PAYMENTS SHOULD BE TOO.

You've found your site, you've had the plans drawn, you've marked out the ground.

Now's the moment when your dream home could become a nightmare.

How on Earth do you find a mortgage? You go to Bradford & Bingley.

We'll give you a Progress Mortgage. It'll pay for your home, and even for the land.

But in stages. So that at any one time you'll only be paying interest on the work so far.

Apart from saving yourself plenty of money, this system helps you think out

your building project stage by stage, so your head can rule your heart.

So if you're thinking of putting together a dream home there's one building you ought to look into. Your nearest Bradford & Bingley.

For full details of Bradford & Bingley mortgages, write to FREEPOST, Bradford & Bingley Building Society, Bingley, West Yorkshire BD16 2LW, or phone free on 0800 252 993. (DTPM)

BRADFORD & BINGLEY
BUILDING SOCIETY

land and build are both paid off with a fresh mortgage, taken out on the completed property. Most people settle for a mortgage equal to the amount they have borrowed, but many lenders will offer a mortgage of anything up to 95 per cent of the property's valuation. If the project has been managed and executed efficiently, the property should be worth considerably more than it has cost to build.

INTEREST AND REPAYMENTS

Interest on finance for individual home-build is usually charged at the lender's standard variable base rate. Although discount rates are traditionally only available on mortgages taken out on the completion of the project, they are now also offered on loans for land or build. Traditionally, banks have charged a higher rate of interest than building societies. However, recent competitiveness in the lending market has encouraged all lenders to charge approximately the same rate.

Repayments on loans for land and build begin as soon as the loan is taken out; however, the repayments on the loan for the build will be small to begin with and then gradually increase as further funds are released. Leading finance schemes are offered by Birmingham Midshires Building Society, Bradford and Bingley, Leeds Permanent and Nationwide Anglia.

BUDGETING

Well-constructed budget plans are an essential part of any individual home-build project. Their primary use is in estimating the total cost of the proposed project, to assess whether it is viable to proceed with it. At a later stage in the project, the budget will form an essential part of negotiations with lenders to secure finance.

The first stage of preparing a budget is to assess the total funds available. For most, this will amount to the total saved or raised from the sale of existing assets, plus the amount that can be borrowed. It is a good idea to talk to lenders offering finance schemes and ask them to explain how they work and to outline how much they would be prepared to lend in principle. Once equipped with an idea of the amount of funds available, it is possible to assess what can be built.

Preparing a budget plan for a building project is like planning a budget for anything else. There are many costs to take into consideration, but the total sum available is finite. To make the figures easier to deal with, it is a good idea to break the costs down into sub-groups of related costs; for example, materials, labour, etc. Approaching budgeting in this simple and straightforward manner makes it easier to account for everything.

When preparing the budget plan, work neatly and clearly. To help avoid confusion, work on a separate sheet of paper for each group of related costs. It is a good idea to open a file in which to keep all written quotations, price lists and contacts. Keep a separate list of telephone numbers for materials suppliers, builders, tradesmen and professionals whose estimated quotes have been worked into the budget. It is easy to forget who quoted the price budgeted for when the time comes to use it.

While preparing the budget, do not be afraid to shop around for good prices and, where possible, get written quotations that are guaranteed for a certain time. When lenders are approached for finance, they will want to see that customers are serious about their intentions. Well-presented plans provide just the right impression.

Also, remember to keep an account of those costs that will have to be met immediately. This is done by getting details of payment and credit terms while asking for estimates. This information will prove invaluable when assessing the amount of cash flow required to meet all current costs during the project.

LAND AND RELATED COSTS

The first cost to budget for is land and the related costs. Besides the price of the plot itself, there will also be the cost of a lender's valuation. This fee cannot usually be added to the loan and so it will have to be paid out of existing funds. The fee is usually around £120–£140, according to the size and value of the plot. There will also be a fee for conveyancing payable to the solicitor; this will again vary according to the size and value of the plot and the amount of work involved. The acquisition of land over £60,000 is also subject to stamp duty at the rate of 1 per cent of the purchase price. This matter is dealt with in the section of this chapter on tax (see page 57).

All these costs are current and therefore will have to be met immediately from available funds.

DIRECT BUILDING COSTS

The next set of costs to contend with are the 'direct building costs'. These are the costs of all the labour and materials needed to complete the project. Those intending to use a builder to undertake all or part of the building work are advised to put the job out to tender and get at least three different quotes.

Those intending to carry out all or part of the work on a DIY basis, or with the help of individual tradesmen, must work out the cost of all the labour and materials separately. There are two ways of employing tradesmen, 'labour only', or on a 'supply and fix' basis.

Supply and fix means the tradesman will supply all the materials required to complete their part of the project within the price they quote. Some trades, such as plasterer, joiner, plumber, etc, are best employed on this basis.

Again, ring around and get some quotes from a number of tradesmen and use these for budget purposes. If a tradesman is worth his salt, he will be prepared to talk about price, on the understanding that he may get the job.

Those intending to undertake any of the trades on a DIY basis, or employ tradesmen on a labour-only basis, must also budget for the necessary materials. This can be done by shopping around a variety of builders' merchants. Alternatively, all the materials required can be bought as a single complete package from a package supplier such as Design and Materials Ltd or RBS Ltd. Many package companies will also create an original design as part of their service and help to budget for the project.

In addition to the cost of labour and materials, those intending to self-manage rather than use a builder must also budget for any plant or machinery required. These costs could include scaffold supply and erection, hire of a cement mixer or even a JCB.

Once all the various costs that come under 'direct building costs' have been estimated, all the sub-totals should be added together and then a contingency of 1 to 2 per cent added to the total. No matter how well all the costs have been budgeted, some unexpected costs can always arise such as the need for special foundations or other unforeseen circumstances.

OTHER COSTS

Lastly come all the other separate groups of related costs involved in a building project, such as the cost of finance, site clearance, external works, connection of utilities, professional fees, and so on.

External works costs

Budget for the building of all pathways around the house, including the driveway and any patios. Those building a detached garage should ensure that they have budgeted for the costs involved in this.

Infrastructure costs

There are also fees payable for building the infrastructure, including connection to the main utilities: water, electricity, telephone and gas (if available). Quotes for infrastructure charges are available from the regional utility offices, namely the Water Board, British Telecom, and so on. Some plots may have no mains sewer within reach and may therefore require septic tank or mini sewage works.

Professional fees

Account for all applicable professional fees; these could include: architect's fees, surveyor's fees, project management fees, structural or civil engineer's fees, planning consultant's fees, local authority inspection fees and fees for any other professional whose services will be required. All these fees are current costs and will have to be paid more or less as they are invoiced.

Finance related costs

It is essential to remember to budget for the cost of finance. This includes the cost of any arrangement fees as well as the cost of repayments to be made during the period of the build. Many lenders will charge a fee for assessing the value of the project when completed. This fee will start at around £120 upwards, according to the size and value of the project. They may also make a similar charge for the valuation of the plot.

Those using a finance scheme that provides funds in stages must also budget for lender's inspection fees on completion of each stage. These fees cannot usually be added to the loan and so will have to be met using available funds. Average re-inspection fees are around £30–£40.

Insurance costs

Do not forget to budget for all the necessary insurances. They will include structural guarantee insurance, arranged through the National House-Building Council (NHBC), essentially an insurance company funded by the volume builders, although it also covers individual projects.

Anyone planning to build their own home other than by using an NHBC registered builder can still arrange a warranty on their home through the Custom Build structural guarantee insurance scheme from Zurich Municipal Insurance, part of the Zurich Insurance Group, one of the world's leading insurers. As with the NHBC scheme, regular

inspections are made of the building work by the insurer's surveyors to ensure that it is in accordance with their own technical requirements, minimising risks and maintaining quality. The completed property is then guaranteed against major damage, which may arise owing to a fault in the structure of the house, for ten years and will refund the cost of any repair work covered by the policy. Cover also includes the cost of alternative accommodation, professional fees, debris removal and the costs of complying with statutory requirements should these ever be necessary during the course of a claim.

Custom Build is available to those building a house using their own skills or employing subcontractors. Those wishing to use the policy simply fill in an application form obtainable from the Building Guarantee Department of Zurich Municipal and return it with a cheque for £100. Providing the project is accepted on to the scheme, the £100 is taken as part payment of the policy. The fee for ten years' cover is a one-off charge starting at around £800 for properties of 800 square feet rising to around £1100 for properties of around 5000 square feet. Once the policy documents have been issued, Zurich Municipal need only 48 hours' notice before work starts to initiate the policy. At the end of the ten years, there is the option to extend the policy by a further five years, subject to claims history and a further premium. Like the NHBC Buildmark policy, the Custom Build policy can be transferred to subsequent purchasers of the property for the duration of the policy. The fee is identical for both timber-frame and brick and block construction.

Alternatively, a form of guarantee can be arranged by using an inspecting architect to issue progress certificates. It is also a good idea to budget for some sort of site insurance to protect against claims for public liability and employer's liability.

Those undertaking any work themselves should also consider budgeting for personal accident cover.

You will also need to budget for building risks insurance. This includes site risks (against theft, vandalism, storm damage and fire), public liability and employers' liability. This essential cover is available as a single convenient policy underwritten by Norwich Union, through DMS Services on 0909 591652. Note that public liability insurance should be taken out as soon as the plot is purchased, to cover against claims from anyone injured on site, including trespassers.

Accommodation costs

Those who have sold or are planning to sell their existing home to help finance the project must not forget to budget for the cost of accommodation during the build.

Planning submission fees

There is a fee payable to the local authority on submission of plans for consideration and this is usually around £110. Building regulation approval must also be arranged by submitting detailed plans to the local authority. The current fee (1994) for this is £72.85.

Value Added Tax

New homes are VAT exempt and therefore it is possible to claim back the VAT on most of the goods and materials that go into the project (see pages 59–60). Remember to include VAT in the budget for cash flow purposes but to subtract it from the estimated 'total project cost'. Remember, though, that any materials provided by builders or other tradesmen on a 'supply and fix' basis will be 'zero rated', as will their labour, and therefore carry no VAT.

TOTAL PROJECT COST

Any additional costs for exceptional items that have not been mentioned so far should be added to the budget where appropriate, such as the cost of building a swimming pool, sauna, tennis courts, fences and compulsory landscaping.

Once the sub-totals for each of the groups of related costs have been established, the total of all the groups will give a very good estimate of the final cost of the proposed project. By comparing the total cost with the available budget, it is possible to assess whether the project is viable or if adjustments need to be made.

If handling all these figures seems complicated, there is a far simpler option. The whole budget process can be handed over to an architect or package supplier. This service is called a 'feasibility study' and is normally carried out for a fixed fee.

Once a realistic and feasible budget has been prepared, it is a good idea to draw up some neat proposals to present to lenders. Remember, though, that there is no point in underestimating building costs just to get approval for finance. This will inevitably lead to problems with cash flow during the build.

CASH FLOW FORECAST

Once detailed budget plans have been prepared, including the collation of all credit and payment terms for each item, this information can be used to develop a cash flow forecast. This is done by first developing a building schedule itemising each stage of the building work and listing all the items in the budget as they will be required. By filling in the details of the schedule on a calendar, the payment dates for each item can then be added according to their payment and credit terms. The net total of these payments in between the release of loan funds will indicate the maximum cash flow requirement at any stage of the project.

TAXATION AND INDIVIDUAL HOME-BUILD

Part of the project planning process includes being aware of the various taxes that are involved in developing a new home. These include stamp duty, Income Tax, Value Added Tax and Capital Gains Tax. The news for individual home-builders is not all bad.

Stamp duty

The first tax likely to be encountered is payable at a rate of 1 per cent, on the acquisition of a building plot or property over £60,000.

Below the threshold there is no stamp duty; however, if the threshold is exceeded by as little as a few pence, the entire sum becomes subject to duty and not just the amount falling over £60,000. Stamp duty is normally paid through the solicitor, as part of the conveyancing costs.

Income tax relief

Those who have borrowed money to buy a plot will be eligible to claim income tax relief on the interest on the first £30,000 of the loan, provided the land was purchased with the intention of building a home on it and the home will be the individual's principal private residence.

Income tax relief on money borrowed for land is claimed under MIRAS (Mortgage Interest Relief at Source), just as it is on an ordinary house purchase loan. To claim MIRAS, a simple application form must be completed. This will usually be provided by the lender. Those eligible for MIRAS do not have to reclaim income tax at the end of the tax year, but will instead receive 'tax relief at source'. This means that the relief will be deducted from their monthly mortgage payment. From April 1994 all credits are at the basic rate of 20 per cent (15 per cent from April 1995), regardless of any higher or lower bracket tax payments. Higher rate tax relief was abolished in the 1991 Budget. Self-employed people who are not on PAYE can still claim MIRAS in the same way.

Claiming MIRAS on an individual home-build project will in no way affect any claim being made against interest payments on an existing home. Even those who purchased their homes before the August 1988 deadline, and are still enjoying double MIRAS on two lots of £30,000, can claim a third £30,000 of relief on a home-build project. They will, however, like everyone else, revert to a single £30,000 of relief when they sell their existing home and move into the new one.

Despite MIRAS strictly being available only on the principal private residence, in other words the main home, MIRAS on an existing property and on an individual home-build project can go on simultaneously for up to three years or until the project is complete. Double MIRAS is also available to anyone who has two properties because they have moved to a new home but are unable to sell the old one. This rule also applies to individual home-builders who are unable to sell their old home when the new one is complete. After the three-year period, extra MIRAS is at the discretion of the Inland Revenue.

If MIRAS is claimed on a piece of land and then the plot is sold on before it is developed, the transaction will be considered an investment and the income tax relief may have to be repaid to the Inland Revenue.

Those developing their project as a home and workplace, and therefore as a part of a business, will be in a different position as regards income tax relief. The position will depend largely on details including design and the proportion of space used solely for work purposes.

The main consideration will be the proportion of the cost of the premises that is allocated to and claimed for under the business. As with all property, if a total of more than two-thirds of the premises is rented out, used for business or any purpose other than providing a home, MIRAS is not applicable. Instead, tax relief will be granted under a combination of allowances for work, rent and an amount of tax relief proportional to the area used solely for accommodation.

Value Added Tax

One of the few items not subject to Value Added Tax is a new home. Individual home-builders can claim back the VAT they pay on most of the materials and goods that go into their new home.

Details are laid out in Customs and Excise Notice 719, entitled 'Refunds of VAT to DIY Home Builders' and is available from your local Customs and Excise VAT office. The information leaflet and related forms are very clear and useful. Only the title might be misleading – there need not be any actual DIY work involved in the project for a claim to be eligible.

The notice states that claims are only allowed for 'complete new dwellings' provided they are not developed as part of a business. This means that no VAT refund is made on conversions, reconstructions, extensions or any other enlargements or improvements to any existing building. Neither is it possible to reclaim VAT for the building of granny annexes, bachelor flats, and so on, which are fully attached to an existing property.

The key to dealing with VAT efficiently is to be aware right from the planning stage what is VAT exempt and what is not. A general guide or rule of thumb is that all items installed as an integral part of the building, ie the structure and fixtures and fittings, are deductible, while any item that can be removed and taken away is not deductible. This means that deductible items include all normal building materials from bricks and blocks to electrical goods, insulating materials, kitchen units and other built-in units and work surfaces (excluding other fitted furniture). Also exempt are less obvious items such as fireplaces and surrounds, curtain rails, wallpaper and paints. Outdoor items such as a detached garage, fencing and walling, paths, driveways and patios are all also VAT exempt, provided they are built at the same time as the dwelling.

Non-exempt items include: all soft furnishings and decorations such as carpets and underlay, curtains and blinds, clocks and lampshades. Also non-deductible are all white goods such as cookers, fridges, freezers and even hobs (although why anyone would want to take their hob with them when they move is another matter!). VAT is also non-refundable on tool hire or purchase or on professional and supervisory services.

These lists are by no means exhaustive, but they do give a good outline as to what is or is not subject to VAT. For any items that fall into a grey area it is well worth contacting the local Customs and Excise VAT office for a ruling. In order to make any claim it is essential that all receipts are kept and this means VAT receipts if possible – no receipt equals no refund.

Receipts must have the supplier's VAT registration number and state the quantity and description of goods and the price of each item. It is also vital to remember everything the first time, as only one claim can be made and it must be made within three months of the completion of the project. To claim, evidence must be provided to prove that the dwelling genuinely exists and is completed. This means providing evidence of planning permission and proof of completion in the form of a completion certificate or letter from an independent architect or surveyor; a certificate of habitation from the local authority; or a certificate from the lender stating that the building is complete.

Once Customs and Excise are satisfied that a claim is valid, they will send a cheque for the refund and return all documentation. A typical refund for a four-bedroom detached house will be £4000–£5000. If part or all of the claim is rejected, a letter will be sent explaining why.

The rejection can be disputed. The first step is to write to the Customs and Excise office, query the rejection and substantiate your claim. If this fails and there is still a dispute, the case can be taken to an independent VAT tribunal. Information about the appeals procedure is given in the leaflet 'Appeals and Applications to the Tribunal', also available from the local Customs and Excise Office.

Capital Gains Tax

Despite the prospect of a healthy 20 to 30 per cent paper gain on a well-planned and efficiently executed project, the Chancellor cannot get his hands on a single penny of it, provided that the new property is the individual's principal private residence and that they live in it for at least 12 months.

There is, however, some degree of flexibility over this rule. For instance, the Chancellor is understanding if someone is left with two properties because they are unable to sell an existing home. The tax inspector is also able to exercise considerable discretion if someone is forced to sell their new home before the 12 months are up, for professional reasons, such as relocation or a new job, or for financial reasons; for example, unemployment or illness.

There are some individual home-builders who go on to build repeatedly, each time living in the new property for one year and meanwhile building another new home. The tax man will tolerate this for only so long before those concerned are 'deemed' to be a developer and are taxed as such.

3500 sq. ft. 4 bedroomed Farm House

Produced by Christian Torsten

CHAPTER 4

FINDING LAND FOR A HOUSE

PAUL GIBBONS

Paul Gibbons is a land consultant with Tailor Made Homes Ltd, a specialist company which provides a comprehensive range of services to private clients who wish to build their own homes. He has many years' experience in the management of residential developments and has worked as a senior manager for some of the country's leading construction companies.

It may be a little unkind to say it, but for many people who first start to think about buying land to build a house for themselves the picture that comes to mind is of a regularly shaped plot, quite flat from one end to the other, fenced, with a few trees (but only on the perimeter, of course), accessed by its own driveway meandering in from a neat tree-lined avenue. It will also be south backing, not overlooked but with spectacular views . . . and with the grass neatly and perpetually cut. No aircraft, trains or roads within earshot and not a pylon in sight. It is all part of the dream of building your own house and no doubt encourages a large number of people to become interested in the idea.

The reality is a little different, and spotting a good plot is one of the great skills of successful individual building. Frequently good plots are not obvious, and securing one involves persistence, an eye for seeing what something will look like when developed, and the ability to push through deals which involve others, because most sites that become available are designated for more than one house.

I was once ticked off in my youth for describing a certain house, which I was particularly impressed with at the time, as being unique. The person I was talking to remarked rather pointedly that *every* house is unique! Over the years I have come to realise the truth of this. It is not so much the design or the presentation of houses − which can be remarkably repetitive − but their situation, the lie of the land and the surroundings.

Despite the exciting potential for home-build, it is necessary to comply with a planning system that polices the status quo, extracts structure plans from local authorities, and generally ensures that it is one of the most difficult bureaucratic obstacle races ever conceived to get permission to build a house.

A field without planning permission is home to cows and corn. A field with planning permission is a building plot, potentially home to you. Transforming the former into the latter can be done but, given the incredible variety of our landscape and history, don't be surprised to find yourself looking at something you are not used to and which is completely unexpected.

Being also a small, economically developed country, we have aircraft, railway lines, roads (or road noise) and pylons almost everywhere, so don't expect to find a site without something slightly wrong with it.

You are never going to find much choice in any one given location and to get an acceptable plot it is necessary to look over a wide area − at least one county, possibly more. Use the communications infrastructure to your advantage; be flexible about location, think in terms of how long you want to spend travelling to work each day instead of how far, look for sites with more than one plot, as well as singles, and you will be surprised at the number and quality of sites available.

Don't get bogged down in too many preconceived ideas about what a plot should or should not be like; judge it on its merits, particularly what it will cost versus what it will be worth, be realistic about what you can afford and what is available, and be prepared to make some compromises on the land, bearing in mind that you will be making fewer compromises on the design and layout because that is something which, in this instance, you have control over.

In identifying land to build a home, the background to the plot is likely to be one of the following:

SINGLE PLOT PREVIOUSLY UNDEVELOPED WITH DIRECT INDEPENDENT ACCESS

Everybody wants one of these and they are as easy to find as the Holy Grail in many areas. Such plots are very scarce because they are easily developed – so most of them already have been. Their introduction to the market is usually prompted by a fundamental change in circumstances, such as an increase in values which proves too tempting for the owner to refuse or, conversely, financial hardship which requires assets previously held in reserve to be sold.

Sometimes people loathe the very idea of developing such sites because they form part of a garden which they enjoy and do not wish to see changed during their lifetime. Although saleable and indeed valuable they are rarely disposed of hastily by their owners.

SMALL IN-FILL DEVELOPMENT OF TWO TO FIVE PLOTS

There are many high quality residential areas which have been developed to particularly low densities and on a piecemeal, random basis. With a small amount of replanning, a substantial increase in the number of houses can be accommodated and a good average plot size of, say, a fifth to a third of an acre can still be maintained, without affecting the overall quality of the area. Local authorities tend to favour this form of development as it enables them to provide services more cost effectively when complete, and more homes can be provided without encroaching on open spaces. Such sites can be ideal, but are rarely undertaken in the self-build sector because the site assembly is invariably a problem.

Developers with cash for option agreements tend to secure them at an early stage, enabling them to arrange a satisfactory planning permission which they can then proceed to build out.

Anyone seriously interested in building their own home should consider forming a consortium in order to bid for sites such as these, or work with someone who can. This is not the easiest way to buy land but such sites can represent good value, or possibly the only way to get what you want where you want it.

SMALL REDEVELOPMENT OF ONE TO FIVE PLOTS

In simple terms any site with an existing building on it is potentially a redevelopment site. Unless the existing building/s is/are listed there is usually no reason why you cannot demolish what is there and replace it with something else. Normally you have a permitted development right to increase the floor area of your building by up to 10 per cent unless there is an overriding reason to refuse permission. If you are in a low density area it may not be at all difficult to increase substantially the number of houses or the amount of building.

The overall constraint tends to be not planning controls but what is viable and what you can afford. For redevelopment to be viable it may require a substantial increase in the amount of building and the number of buildings, say, from one large family house to a block of flats – which is of no interest to self-builders.

There are, however, many instances of quite low-grade and relatively low-priced houses sitting on superb plots of possibly an acre or more where the land value, if you can get a good enough house on it, is equal to, if not higher than, the value of the existing house. If the figures do not add up for one house, an application to increase unit density will normally be supported by the planners so long as it is not excessive. Legal covenants restricting development also need to be checked.

Again, there is clearly a difficulty here in that the site may be larger or more expensive than most people would want for themselves so the formation of a consortium may need to take place.

As a general rule of thumb guide to density, 1000 square feet of habitable floor space per one-tenth of an acre is not an unreasonable expectation where two-storey buildings are permissible.

MULTI-PLOT SITES

An area of land with planning permission or potential for two or more houses is called a 'multi-plot site', and such plots constitute by far the majority of building plots that become available. They are not necessarily 'high density'; they can, in fact, be very low density, providing self-contained and secluded positions.

They just happen to become available as more than one plot for the simple reason that legally they have not yet been divided up, and the vendor is only interested in completing a single transaction.

In some instances they may have an existing independent and direct access; on other occasions a road and infrastructure may need to be built in order to serve the site. It is obviously more complex if a road and services have to be punched through, but that in itself is no reason for dismissal. All sites should be judged entirely on their merits in terms of value for money and suitability to your own aspirations.

In order to provide anything like sufficient land to the self-build market, there has to be a supply of multi-plot sites, otherwise the price of individual single plots would be forced up by excessive demand – sadly there are just not enough single plots to go round.

Multi-plot sites tend to come available in the following ways:

(a)   A developer buys a site, puts in infrastructure and sells the plots individually for the highest possible price. This is usually done to improve cash flow and to ease up on borrowings, perhaps enabling the builder to complete another part of the site on a fully speculative basis.

(b)   Housing associations sometimes buy sites with outside finance for self-build groups physically to build homes for themselves. Institutions have become increasingly reluctant to fund this type of project in recent times because of difficulties in imposing a discipline, particularly from the point of view of timing.

(c)   Consortia of individuals increasingly buy sites with each member responsible for finance. Each member is fully contracted in from the outset with a vested interest between all parties in ensuring a successful outcome. There are specialist project management teams who are able to form groups together successfully and co-ordinate and manage the finance to make this kind of approach work very effectively.

The demand for management expertise in this instance is extremely high, but if planned and executed professionally this method provides all the advantages of having a developer sort out the problems while the client still has a tailor-made home and – as the principal source of finance – the developers profit.

HOW DO YOU VALUE A PLOT?

It is often said that land has a value set as a percentage of the value of the completed house. The much quoted 'one third, one third and one third' rule – one third for land, one third for building and one third for profit – is a typical example. Such edicts are meaningless if not highly dangerous and should not be relied upon. That is not to say that land cannot be worth a third; sometimes it is.

Sometimes, if you have an exceptionally high valued area and your development costs are low, land values can be considerably more. Conversely, if you are in a low valued area, a few problems with the ground and getting services in can mean the land may even have a negative value; it will cost more to develop than it is worth.

Another time-honoured and equally misleading formula is to work purely on market prices. 'If plot A has sold for £100,000 then plot B must be worth the same if it is substantially similar.' This may be quite a reasonable, if not the only, method of valuing a house but building plots are not the same and this approach does not take into account the fact that some people buy land without doing their arithmetic first, or without knowing how to do the arithmetic, preferring instead to value by comparison.

After all it is easier, it saves time, it does afford some measure of comfort to know that you are not the only one in the world who can get mugged and the blind may indeed prefer to be led by the blind!

Valuations in general terms of X or Y per acre are again quite useless. The value of land is not determined by how large that piece of land is or by any other simplistic formula but by:

(a) What you can put on it
(b) What the value of the building/s is going to be
(c) How much it costs to put it there
(d) What you need to allow for risk and profit margin
(e) Whether there is a better deal on offer.

Before proceeding to buy a plot it is vital that all these items are thoroughly checked and that you have the right answers. Unfortunately, the answers are not always obvious and it requires skill to get it right.

Most people underestimate the complexity behind these questions, fail to take expert advice, allow far too little money for building, pay far too much for their plot and thereby ultimately contribute to inflating the land market.

As the success of the project as a whole is determined by each of the many component parts, it is important to seek advice from someone who is actively involved and experienced in all these elements and not just one isolated part of the story.

Either qualified surveyors with a building and valuation capability or project managers who specialise in housing are likely to be the most helpful. Timber-frame manufacturers can offer advice within their own immediate sphere but are unlikely to be able to offer much help with regard to land or in producing a fully comprehensive budget and site appraisal.

In terms of budgets, the golden rule is believe what someone quotes you for something they directly supply or do; be wary of what anybody quotes you for something they do not do. If you want to know the price of bread ask the baker not the milkman.

Having identified a plot in the right place and one that you can afford, do not take it for granted that just because you can afford it you are necessarily getting good value, or that all the costs will work out the way you want them to. Assuming that you can get the sort of house that you want on the plot it is important to establish exactly what all your costs are going to be, firstly from the point of view of building.

Whatever anyone says, there are two things you must know about building costs:

(a) There is no such thing as a standard build cost
(b) There is no such thing as a truly fixed build cost.

Remember, the whole object of the exercise is to get away from standard volume housing in order to get something which is specially built for you, so don't expect instantaneous 'cast in stone' figures on costs.

Nobody can tell you exactly what it will cost until you know exactly what you want; in this regard timber-frame structures are of tremendous help because they enable you effectively to fix the price of a substantial element of the building at a relatively early date, and also afford greater flexibility with regard to where you put the walls with minimal need for additional reinforcement and late variations on cost.

Prior to exchanging contracts it is possible, with the benefit of a soil test combined with a timber-frame quote, to get a very reliable figure for all your substructures and superstructures, which are cost areas you normally have little control over.

Internal finishes are almost infinitely variable in accordance with your budget and aspirations. But once you have a confirmed figure for professional and planning fees, legal costs and stamp duty, and by using estimates for build cost, the cost of finance can be calculated. This provides a check on what you are paying for the land. A Residual Land Value (RLV) can then be calculated.

Example:
2000 square feet house. Five bedrooms, two bathrooms, four reception rooms, double garage. Decorated, cleaned out and ready to furnish.

Home counties area. No adverse conditions. Serviced plot.

Value of house when completed:		£250,000
Less cost to build:	£100,000	
Less finance, legal, design:	£10,000	
Less margin or saving, 20 per cent:	£50,000 (£160,000)	
RESIDUAL LAND VALUE		**£90,000**

Before completing this exercise you should have a valuation in hand from a surveyor on the value of the completed house. In most cases this will need to be done in order to raise finance or may have been organised on your behalf by your lender.

If you have to pay substantially more than your calculated RLV in order to get the vendor to settle, it is then a simple matter of deciding how much of the margin you are prepared to forgo and this may also depend on what other alternative plots are available at the time. If there are equally good opportunities on the market at a lower price, it could be worthwhile offering a lower figure.

The important thing to bear in mind is that there are no fixed rules about land values but it is important to develop your own guidelines to arrive at a sensible figure. You pay what you think it is worth to you and at a level which will enable you to look forward realistically to a successful outcome.

BUDGETING – YOUR TIME AND YOUR MONEY

It is perfectly possible to be quoted a vast array of different 'all inclusive' costs for building a house ranging from £30 to £35 per square foot at the bottom end of the scale, to anything up to £70 to £80 per square foot at the top end. Off-the-cuff estimates – anything which is not defined by a detailed plan and specification – are in essence unreliable, but there is certainly a great deal of confusion in many people's minds and regrettably it is all too easy to be misled.

All things being equal, building costs depend on whether you are going to build fully and manage the project yourself, or have professionals complete the entire job for you and, if you are using timber-frame, whose timber-frame you select. But it is not altogether as simple as that.

If you are just contemplating managing the building of the house yourself it will involve an enormous commitment in time which is all too easy to underestimate. Physically building it as well is most definitely a full-time job unless you see it as a hobby for many years to come. Every month journals produce case studies of people who have given up work for two years to complete the job. Great, if that is really all you want to do, but if by doing it you sacrifice two years' income at, say, £25,000 p.a. the house should have at least a £50,000 surcharge against it purely for loss of income without taking into account loss of pension rights or any other perks. How often do people allow for this time in the accompanying budget?

In working through projects with clients, people frequently find it difficult just to find the time to select the design and layout they want and it is not at all unusual for people to spend days on end agreeing their final specification. So, even if someone is managing the whole project for you, don't underestimate the time you will want to spend getting everything the way you want it and checking prices and delivery for the multitude of choices that have to be made. In considering a budget make sure that the following are included:

- Site clearance and preparation

- Foul and surface water drainage
- Service connections
- Paths, driveway, patio, fencing, landscaping
- Garage
- Kitchen units
- Wardrobes
- Site insurance and National House-Building Council (NHBC) insurance
- Temporary storage and wc facility
- Time to manage the build and deal with administration and supervision
- Safety and safety precautions. You have legal obligations.

A reasonably reliable guide to include all these items at 1993 prices is £50 per square foot, taking the sum total of all the building and dividing the cost into the habitable floor space measured across the inside of the external walls.

This assumes a good contemporary standard of specification, standard foundations and that the house has at least 1800 square feet of habitable accommodation. Smaller houses will increase this rate as there is less economy of scale and bungalows will always (all things remaining equal) cost more.

The above definition of a square foot is the nearest thing to an industry standard we have. Sometimes costs are divided back over the total gross area which includes the width of the external walls and garages which will obviously produce a lower square foot price. When square foot prices are quoted always check on the basis of the square foot.

WHAT CAN YOU DO WITH THE SITE?

There are an infinite number of ways to spoil a good site. Sometimes the most unpromising sites can be turned into excellent developments. A piece of land should never be looked at simply as what it is but as what you can make of it. If there is a point at which people go wrong it is in their lack of ability, training, experience: in a word vision, to see what can be done.

Some people will spend an age looking for that perfect site that stands out from the rest, not find anything and then blame it on a lack of sites. Others will spend very little time, buy the most unpromising of plots at a knock-down price and create a wonderful home.

The important thing is to think through what you want to do and not hesitate in making best use of the excellent professional help which is at hand. Find an architect who is genuinely interested in individual houses and who is prepared to spend time working through your ideas in sketch form, taking into account the site's natural characteristics of orientation, levels and vistas.

For a quite modest fee architects will do a considerable amount of groundwork to help you get the right result and going through this exercise will not only help to give a clearer vision of what you can achieve but also provide a sound basis for working out a budget on that particular site. Once you have the facts and figures, you can then gain confidence and the rest becomes a lot easier.

Determining what you can put on a site is not always straightforward. It might well be that what you want could be quite different from what has been previously envisaged. Planning officers will not be able to give you reliable advice without you giving them reliable information, and you may run up against a certain amount of prejudice following on from previous applications.

LOCATION, LOCATION AND LOCATION

As the time-honoured phrase goes, these are the three essential ingredients that must be right and without them it doesn't matter, even if you want to build Buckingham Palace, if it is in the wrong place; don't count on anyone else wanting to live there.

Selecting a plot is very much a matter of personal preference, but it is also important when you buy land to keep a sense of perspective about its investment value and to select a plot which is not only right for you but also right for the type of building you want to put on it.

Developers talk in terms of 'optimising' sites, which means putting the right size, style and mix of houses on to any given location in order to yield the overall best return on investment.

In building your own home it is probably not a good idea to let this become the be-all and end-all, but if you want to ensure that you have a

Create the right Impression

The first thing you notice about the Fujitsu air conditioners is their stylish good looks.

The second thing you notice is how their soft, smooth lines merge into the background of any environment. That way you end up looking at the genuine works of art.

And like most works of art, the longer you treasure it the more you discover how much more there is than meets the eye.

The clean functional design disguises the most advanced micro electronic technology that only a company such as Fujitsu could possibly provide.

Multi directional airflow adjustment, instant air exchange, reverse cycle heating system, wired and infra-red remote controls.

Just some of the advanced features to be found in the attractive, unobtrusively styled Fujitsu range.

The super-quiet 'heating and cooling' range from Fujitsu. *Creating the right impression...*

Ceiling mounted

Cassette Unit

Wall mounted

Window mounted

For further information phone 0707 272841 or write to Fujitsu General (U.K.) Co. Limited. 154 Great North Road, Hatfield, Herts AL9 5JN

good investment, buying a large expensive plot in order to build a small inexpensive house is unlikely to produce a satisfactory result.

'This is the heart of the district. Every plot is a stone's throw from the station. As soon as you throw enough stones we are going to build a station.' (Groucho Marx)

Also be wary when people claim that changes in communications will necessarily bring dramatic increases in house and land values. For one thing, it might never happen, and for another, some of the lowest value areas in the country are in fact located within the proximity of principal road and rail links. Value is all to do with supply and demand, nothing else. If demand is likely to increase, supply can react likewise – sometimes quicker than many people think.

RESEARCH – A BASIS FOR NEGOTIATION

In looking for a plot of land, the need to research the market thoroughly cannot be understated. The problem is that the market is highly fragmented, there are many agents who sell a plot occasionally but few who specialise and do it all the time. Some are not always known to the general public as they prefer to deal with a select number of contacts in the trade rather than spend time and money on advertising. So it is never easy for people to get information which will enable them to build up a reliable picture in their own mind of what is really on offer.

Unlike a house, land is not quite so easy to put a price on because, as previously discussed, it is worth different sums to different people.

The essential points that you need to compare are:

(a) *Location*
What are the surrounding properties like and worth, and is there anything, such as aspect/view or the proximity of the local sewage works, which might have a particular effect on value?

(b) *Frontage*
Width of plot is a critical factor in determining the style of house. A quarter acre plot 60 feet wide should be worth far more than a half acre plot 35 feet wide, simply because a 35 feet wide plot is inadequate for a full double-fronted house.

(c)   *Planning constraints*

Sometimes the size of house may be limited by height ('must be a bungalow'), or by a green belt restriction which limits the size of any new building to no more than was there previously. In this instance the plot is probably going to be worth less than it would be without such limitations. Vendors are often reluctant to accept this.

It is surprising how often agents fail to report in their details the physical dimensions of a site, or other vital planning constraints.

As a way of comparing one site with another, it can be helpful to divide the price by the amount of accommodation you can put on the site in order to give you the price for the land per square foot of accommodation. In carrying out this analysis on over 1000 sites during the last three years in the south east of England there has been a variation of between £30 per square foot to over £90 per square foot. This tends to confirm the notion many people have that the variation in vendors' expectations are far greater in the land market than in the normal house market.

It also indicates that the quality of advice given to vendors is not what it should be or that land-owners do not always listen to the advice being offered. It is nowhere near as easy to compare one piece of land with another as it is to compare one house with another, because the value of land is in what you do with it. Vendors have a tendency to aim high to start with and try to get a feel for what someone might be prepared to pay by way of trial and error.

An agent needs to make an accurate assessment of what you can do with a site and by doing so is able to advise on what it is worth, but he will also be fully aware that it is not always easy to persuade a client to accept his advice.

This air of scepticism and uncertainty which vendors often have is the reason why so many pieces of land are offered for sale by tender, auction or an 'offers invited in the region of' basis – it is the result of an agent saying, 'Well, this is my advice but if you are not entirely convinced, put it to the market and see.'

Getting a good deal is very much a matter of being in the right place at the right time, knowing a bargain when you see one and being in a position to act. This is not simply a matter of luck. It is a matter of skill, research and persistence.

To start with, find out as much information as possible about suitable sites for sale and go out and see as many as you can. Do not disregard a site because it seems too expensive; make an offer at what you think is the right price and if it is rejected keep it on file. Keep a watch on it to see what happens and make sure that your bid is not forgotten. Do this enough times and eventually you will 'get lucky' and opportunities will come your way; the important thing is being able to take advantage of them when they do. In this world you make your own luck.

However, if the place where you are going to live is more important to you than simply making money out of the deal, you may have to pay a premium to get what you want.

MARKET OVERVIEW

At the moment the market is showing signs of recovery. The land market is frequently seen to move ahead in anticipation of a rise in house prices. Many sites which have been on the market for up to two or three years have sold in the last 12 months. Liquidator sales are well past their peak and there are now generally fewer new plots being offered than being sold. The major housebuilders are all gearing up again and there is likely to be a real scarcity of land.

During the recession land values fell considerably more than house prices. This restricted the supply of new land into the market. As prices pick up, land-owners will be attracted into the market as development or redevelopment becomes an attractive option once again.

STARTING YOUR SEARCH

I can only point others in the same directions I have always looked, which are principally: planning application registers and local structure plans (to see what is likely to become available in the future), local and national newspapers which are known for property advertising, *Build It!* and *Individual Homes*, specialist publications aimed at the property industry such as *Estates Times* and *Estates Gazette*, estate agents, receivers and liquidators, other housebuilders, architects, surveyors, what is already under your own nose, and, last but not least, your own eyes and common sense.

CHAPTER 5

THE PLANNING SYSTEM AND WORKING WITH AN ARCHITECT

DUNCAN MATHEWSON

Duncan Mathewson is an architect, a partner at Mathewson Whittaker Architects and a director of Four Square Design Ltd. He trained at Brighton and has been in practice for 18 years, building up considerable experience negotiating with local authorities on behalf of private clients.

If you have decided to build your own individual home, you may find the planners either infuriatingly obstructive or incredibly helpful.

There are a few basic rules and guidelines which should be followed when applying for planning permission from the local council, and there are advantages in dealing through an architect who will be familiar with the planning system. There is little variation between local authorities, which process applications according to standard procedures.

To those who have not previously encountered the working of the planning department, the ways in which planning permissions are either approved or refused can sometimes be something of a mystery. Decisions to grant or refuse planning applications are made by committees of district councillors, usually around 12 or 14, who meet on average once a month in the council chamber.

For each application the councillors will have a recommendation from the planning officer, which advises them either to refuse or approve the application. Each proposal is, in theory, discussed and usually – but not always – the planning officer's recommendation is followed by the committee.

To be successful in gaining planning permission for your self-build house means that in practice you have to convince the planning officer that the scheme you are proposing is acceptable. If for some reason he is unhappy with the proposal you can try to bypass him, but that involves successful lobbying of the committee, which is difficult and unpredictable.

It is advisable to contact the planners informally before submitting the application, to get their initial reaction to your scheme. A meeting on your site with the area planning officer can be most useful, as any potential problems, such as suitability of access or the style of the proposed house, can then be dealt with before the application is submitted.

Even after the application has been registered it is still possible to overcome either planners' or local residents' objections to the scheme by amending the proposal before a decision is reached. Where possible, it is worth obtaining any informal views expressed by the planner in writing, particularly if they are favourable, so that you have a record of any comments.

Having submitted your application, it will take on average eight weeks for the council to make a decision. This allows time for a site notice to be displayed (usually for 14 or 21 days) and for consultations with the local parish or town council, the county surveyor or local highway engineer. Their comments will be taken into account by the planning officer and reported to the committee. It partly explains why they usually require at least four copies of the plans.

The planning officer in charge of your application will prepare a report, making recommendations to put before his committee after about six weeks. If the recommendation is for refusal, it may be a simple matter of changing a detail or making a comparatively minor alteration to change the recommendation. If, however, you are unable to deal with the problem and disagree with the planner it may then be helpful to arrange to meet your local district councillor on site. This will give you an opportunity to explain why you think the local authority planners are wrong to oppose your scheme and to say why you think permission should be granted.

You may be successful in persuading the councillor to support your proposal; you will then have a representative on the committee who may oppose the recommendation to refuse the application. On average, a planning committee will ignore their officer's advice on 10 to 15 per cent of the applications put before them at a meeting.

Some councils now allow members of the public or their agents to speak at meetings during the consideration of their application. Those who oppose an application will also, under these circumstances, be permitted to put their side of the argument. Your local authority can advise you as to whether they operate this scheme.

Occasionally, planning committees will defer consideration of an application and arrange a site visit. This can often help your case; councillors can be lobbied to ensure that they are fully aware of all the relevant facts and that they appreciate your side of the argument.

Negotiating a successful application can often be very time-consuming and this may be one further reason for employing an architect and, in some special cases, a planning consultant or even a highway consultant if, for example, there is difficulty with access. Whether successful or not, the local authority will issue a Notice of Decision either granting consent, in which case conditions would be attached, or refusal, where the reasons will be set out on the form.

TYPES OF PLANNING APPLICATION

Planning applications may be submitted in 'outline' form or as a full planning application. The first method is often advisable to determine the principle of the proposal. Since one can by no means be certain that consent will be granted for a house on any particular site, an outline planning application is usually the first stage.

In addition to the 2cm to 1km scale maps with which we are all familiar

(1:50,000), Ordnance Survey produce detailed maps of the whole of the country to a scale of 1:2500 and in some cases, particularly towns, 1:1250. These show all houses, boundaries, roads, paths, and so on, in sufficient detail to identify your site.

You may submit the application whether or not you own the site, provided the owner is formally notified, but in the first instance a visit to the local council is advisable, because there may already exist on file a planning history in relation to the site.

Often, a site will be sold with the benefit of outline consent for a dwelling, and details of exactly what the council have approved can be inspected. It is rarely worth considering purchasing a site without outline planning consent, although it may be possible to make the purchase 'subject to consent being granted'.

The Official Notice of Consent will contain any conditions which apply and must be observed. Outline consent is valid for three years from the date of the approval and detailed consent for five years. Often there is a restriction on the size of the dwelling, referred to in square metres as the gross floor area.

No work can proceed until details of design, siting, access, landscaping, etc, have been approved. This will take the form of a so-called Reserved Matters application. Effectively, this is the same as a full or detailed planning application, with the exception that the basic principle of a dwelling on that site is not in question.

The cost of preparing an outline application is considerably cheaper than a detailed application which illustrates the final form you propose your house to take, although the planning fee is usually the same and can, under certain circumstances, be higher.

PREPARING AND SUBMITTING PLANNING APPLICATIONS

The groundwork and preparation, together with the quality of the presentation of your application, is most important. All too often, applications are poorly presented with insufficient information for the application to be even registered.

You will find that the application form provided by your local authority will be accompanied by a set of guidance notes stating the fees – which vary – and the form in which the application must be presented, together with the number of copies required.

It is customary with a full or detailed application for the drawing or drawings to include floor plans, elevations, a site plan and a location plan as a minimum requirement. If it appears that the proposed location for a new house is likely to be contentious, it is helpful to provide perspectives showing the building in relation to its surroundings. Water-colour drawings may also assist, especially if presented to the planning committee, who would then have before them attractive, well-presented proposals, which may even put them in the right frame of mind for granting permission.

It is important to keep in touch with the progress of your application and find out the date of the planning committee meeting and the planning officer's recommendation to the committee. Any objections raised, either by local residents or, for example, the highways authority, can often be resolved by submitting amendments to the application before a decision is reached. If time is short, it may be possible to defer the decision until amended plans have been submitted. This will delay the application by a further three weeks or a month, but may be sufficient to reverse a negative recommendation.

DESIGN PROBLEMS AND PLANNING PERMISSION

Whether or not a particular house is appropriate for the proposed site is often a matter of personal taste. It is here that one can come up against the planner's own personal views. There are, however, some basic guidelines which can be followed when it comes to trying to get permission.

In certain areas of old towns and villages, local councils have designated conservation areas. These are areas of housing, or perhaps the whole centre of a village, where there are a number of attractive, traditional houses and it is important that any new housing is particularly sensitively designed, so as to fit unobtrusively into the surroundings. Even if the site is not in a conservation area, national park or area of outstanding natural beauty, the planners will still scrutinise very carefully the design of any house which is prominent in the street scene, or in an area where there is uniformity in the design of the existing houses.

Design has always been controversial, and as far as house builders are concerned, planners have a reputation for meddling in the design of their houses. There has been a backlash against what many saw as excessive interference. It was argued that design was such a subjective matter that it should be left to the builders and their architects to be the best judges of what was right or wrong on a particular site. Understandably, the planners took umbrage at this, but eventually the government produced an uneasy compromise, in the form of guidelines on design, published in March 1992.

The advice in these guidelines is fairly predictable, but they are a useful reference point in trying to resolve any argument that you might be having with a planner over the design of your new house.

The advice suggests that obviously poor designs which are out of scale or character with their surroundings should be rejected, but that on the other hand planners should not impose their taste on applications for planning permission simply because they believe it to be superior.

Applicants for planning permission are advised to demonstrate that they have considered the wider setting of their new house, although the guidelines say that house designs should not necessarily mimic the character of their surroundings. The government guidelines also say it can be helpful to submit a short written statement setting out the design principles of the proposals.

PLANNING APPEALS

If the council refuses permission the applicant still has the right of appeal against this decision. The reasons for refusal will be given on the Notice of Decision.

On the back of the Notice of Decision will be advice on how to appeal. This basically involves filling in yet another set of forms, and sending everything off to the Department of the Environment in Bristol, where it will be reconsidered by an independent inspector.

Before deciding to appeal, several points need to be considered. Most importantly, is it worth your while appealing, given the time delay and the additional costs likely to be involved? Or is the council in fact right to refuse your proposal?

It may be worth consulting a specialist town planner for guidance on whether or not to proceed with an appeal. On average only about 30 per cent of appeals each year are successful, and a council will usually win two out of three appeals made against their decisions. The quickest method of appeal, known as the Written Representations procedure, can take up to five months from beginning to end.

Rather than appeal against the decision, it may well be better to discuss with the local authority ways in which your scheme could be amended in order to resubmit the application. This could perhaps take only three months and planning officers are used to being approached in this way following refusals.

The cost of the appeal should also be considered. Fees for employing a planning consultant can range from £1000 upwards, depending on the type of appeal, the complexity of the case and whether additional consultants, or even a solicitor, are required.

Assuming that you have decided to proceed, you have three possible ways of appealing.

1.   The simplest and quickest involves writing out your case and sending it to the Department of the Environment (DoE). The local authority then prepares a similar case to justify their refusal of permission. The inspector from the DoE reads the evidence and arranges to meet you on the site, although this is not an opportunity to discuss the proposal with him. He then goes away and decides either to overrule the council and grant the necessary permission, or to dismiss your appeal.

2.   The second option, called the Informal Meeting procedure, involves attending a meeting at the town hall with the planning officer and the inspector, and debating the merits or otherwise of your case. This is quite a good system, as it gives you a chance to state your case in person and also ensures that the inspector is fully aware of your case. Do not forget that those who have objected may also attend.

3.   The final method of appeal is the Public Enquiry procedure, which in so far as individual plots or small groups of houses are concerned is often inappropriate. It is a system which is more suited to complicated cases, and the proceedings can often go on for days. The inquiry takes place at the town hall, and both you and the council are legally represented.

The procedure is very formal, with cross-examination and evidence given by expert witnesses. This system has the highest success rate (averaging 55 per cent), but can take the best part of a year from beginning to end.

The outcome of planning appeals is by no means certain; however, they are a useful safety net for people who have been refused permission. Provided you can justify the time and extra cost involved, it is often worthwhile considering the appeal procedure.

BUILDING REGULATIONS

Having successfully negotiated the planning hurdles, a building regulations application or notice is required before any work can commence on site. This means that you will have to notify the local authority in whose area the work will be carried out.

Building work must comply with the regulations, which are intended to ensure the health and safety of people using the building, its durability and energy conservation. These were formally set out in a legal document which was not easy to understand and was widely open to interpretation. They were substantially revised in 1985, and were published as a series of 'Approved Documents' by HMSO. The building regulations were further updated in 1991 and came into operation on 1 June 1992, introducing amendments and additional requirements.

All new buildings or alterations must conform with the details and recommendations contained in Documents A, B, C, D, E, F, G, H, J, K, L, M, N and Regulation 7, which together go to make up the best part of a large box file.

As with the planning application, the building regulations application is submitted to the local authority; again an application fee is required, which this time includes VAT.

The cost of a single new house 'plans fee' is currently £72.85, with an inspection fee of £122.20, invoiced following the building inspector's first site visit. The building inspectors have five weeks to consider the application and it is not unusual for an extension of two weeks to be requested. At the end of that period they must either approve or refuse the application, although during the processing period a standard form will usually be sent to the agent where further information is required. Provided this is dealt with within the period, all should be well.

In addition to the architect's drawings, structural details and calculations will be required for sizes of beams, purlins, roof structure and in some cases foundations. Again, the local authority has to approve these and often employs its own consultants.

WORKING DRAWINGS, SCHEDULES AND SPECIFICATION

These are a development of the technical details contained in the building regulation drawings and have to convey more comprehensive information to the contractor. This includes details regarding dimensions, as well as how to set the building out on the site, and the finished floor level relative to existing and proposed ground levels.

The schedules and specification effectively contain a 'shopping list' of all the parts needed to complete the construction of your house, from the type of brick to the locks and latches.

The specification also includes details of the proposed building contract, clauses on workmanship and materials, and for a typical house will extend to anything from 50 to 100 typed pages. With the complete set of drawings the specification will form part of the tender documentation sent to competing contractors.

Competitive tenders

While you may negotiate with a local contractor to carry out the work, it is often best to get a number of detailed quotations. Your architect will have experience of a variety of good local contractors and personal recommendation is the best way of preparing a list of, say, three to six.

All the drawings, schedules and specifications should be packaged up with an identical letter to each of the competing contractors stating the tender period. Most contractors will need to get prices from their suppliers and domestic subcontractors, so a period of three to four weeks will usually be needed. Each company or individual tenderer should be offered the opportunity to visit the site to establish the extent of the work, as well as any constraints. It is customary for the tenders to be returned in marked envelopes, to be opened at a particular time on the specified day at the architect's office.

The quotations are likely to vary enormously, demonstrating the advantage of seeking prices from more than one contractor; however, you are not obliged to accept either the lowest or any of the tenders. Nevertheless, if the selected list of contractors has been carefully chosen, there should be no reason why, subject to checking the lowest tender, it should not be accepted.

In view of the complexity involved in preparing a quotation there is always the possibility that mistakes have been made, either arithmetically or by omission. It is prudent, therefore, to request a breakdown of the contractor's tender calculations, particularly if there is a considerable difference between the lowest and second tenders. Although you are not responsible for checking a quotation, it does neither party any good to discover a mistake halfway through the building programme.

Contract and administration

Having decided to accept a quotation the contractor has to be formally appointed, while the others are thanked and notified. As with any other business arrangement, a formal contract between yourself as employer and the contractor as employee is vital.

The construction industry has prepared a number of different contracts relating to the size and type of the project, issued by the Joint Contracts Tribunal (JCT).

Where an architect is involved, the JCT Agreement for Minor Building Works is normally the most appropriate. It is a comparatively small, well-written document that sets out the conditions by which both parties should abide and includes the contract documents, the sum, the dates for commencement and completion, together with liquidated damages for non-completion.

The 'Control of the Works and Payment' refers to the architect's instructions, certificates of payment, insurance, and so on, so that everyone involved should be aware of their obligations to one another.

WHY USE AN ARCHITECT?

Remarkably few private houses built in Britain have been designed by an architect. Use one and you could create a house that is elegant, practical and in tune with your needs.

Like other professionals architects are there to interpret their clients' requirements, but it would certainly be unfair to hold the architectural profession responsible for many of the gloomy housing estates dotted around the countryside.

Most developers have built up a collection of basic styles over the years which have become a series of standard designs, often given relatively grand names. In our wish to become home-owners, we have perhaps not been quite as discriminating as our European counterparts. Often the only opportunity to individualise a new home is to choose the colour of the tiles and the bathroom suite.

Increasingly, if not wishing actually to build their own house with their bare hands, people are seeking far greater involvement in the design and construction process. As this is the largest single investment that most people will undertake, professional advice is important to ensure the best possible end result and value for money. Architects' lengthy, extensive training (seven years) covers all aspects of building and design, from initial sketch schemes to the management of the building team and supervision of the contract/building work.

Remember that architects are not just people who draw plans and organise the construction of buildings. As well as assisting in the preparation of your brief, they can interpret your requirements in a number of different ways to produce a stimulating home that is enjoyable, practical and appropriate to your family. With comprehensive documentation, a detailed specification and working drawings submitted to a number of contractors for competitive quotations, the difference in building costs alone may well cover the architect's fees.

Recognising an architect

All architects, like doctors, are registered, and the majority are members of the Royal Institute of British Architects (RIBA). This professional institution has a strict code of conduct by which architects must abide and they have a duty of responsibility to their clients, the profession and to society. The term 'architect' is protected and anyone claiming to be one who is not professionally qualified is breaking the law, although the government has indicated that it intends to change this. Architects have a 'duty of care' and are accountable in law for the way they carry out their duties.

Selecting an architect

A *Directory of Architectural Practices* is produced each year. The RIBA also runs a clients' advisory service which is completely free, and it can assist in directing you to a suitable architect by providing a shortlist of practices in your area for the type of project you are considering.

There is, however, no substitute for personal recommendation. In view of the importance of the project to you it is worthwhile taking the time to interview a number of architects and, having drawn up your own shortlist, to arrange to visit recently completed houses. While they may not be to your particular taste, a short discussion with the owner will determine how successful they feel their architect has been in interpreting their wishes.

A project can often last between one and two years from inception to completion and moving in. It should be an enjoyable and rewarding time and a good working relationship between you and your architect is most important for the successful completion of a project.

Each family has different requirements; make sure that yours are as much a part of the 'brief' as the schedule of rooms. A celebrated American architect went so far as to move in with his clients in order, he says, to get to know their lifestyle and to develop a comprehensive 'brief'. Having identified an architect with whom you feel you can work (though not necessarily live!) he or she should provide you with a letter of appointment.

Appointing an architect

Your architect should have an extremely useful guide which is often referred to as the *Blue Book*. This has been prepared by the RIBA to provide a clear understanding of the nature of the services that can be provided and the responsibilities of those involved. In most cases, the *Architect's Appointment – Small Works* edition is the most appropriate, and comprises four sections as follows:

Part 1   Architect's services
Part 2   Other services
Part 3   Conditions of appointment
Part 4   Recommended fees and expenses

Practices will have different letters of appointment which will vary in format but should contain details of the project, extent of the work (either partial or full service), the fees, whether other consultants will be involved and what their fees are likely to be, a programme stating when information is required, the approximate time likely to be involved at each stage: design, planning, building regulations, competitive quotations and contract or building period.

A simple letter accepting these terms, together with, I suggest, a countersigned copy of the architect's letter, is sufficient. You may, in addition, be asked to sign a fee proposal statement or a 'standard' RIBA appointment form. Remember to quote from the 'Blue Book': 'the Architect's appointment may be terminated by either party, on the expiry of a reasonable notice given in writing'.

The brief

This is essentially a list of your requirements and could include sketches, photographs, room details and approximate sizes together with an idea of the finishes both internally and externally. For example, you may wish to have open fires in some rooms, or an Aga, a special form of heating, additional insulation, energy conservation features or have a particular form of construction in mind.

It is helpful for the relationship of the rooms to be considered both with one another and with the outside. Most houses have a public as well as a private face; one often seeks privacy, away from the street side, which is possible when the house opens on to the garden. Given good weather, this can, in the form of conservatories or patios, extend your living space and the enjoyment of your home and garden.

The appearance of a house can often be dictated by adjoining properties or, if the site is more rural, by the typical architecture of the area. The planning authority is usually keen to see this recognised in the design. Nevertheless, it is useful to take photographs of houses, parts of houses or styling details that you would like to see incorporated.

Your architect should be able to prepare sketch schemes based on the information that you have provided in order for the initial design process to begin. Do not worry if your ideas are not realised immediately in the first scheme; it will serve as a useful basis for discussion and for the generation of the next scheme. Gradually, the scheme will evolve with you refining the details as the plans and elevations take shape.

Usually, these will be drawn to a scale of either 1:100 or in some cases 1:50, as all plans are expected to be submitted in metric scales. Conversion scale rules to feet and inches are available and it is still the case that most people, and many architects, prefer imperial dimensions, particularly in domestic work. We have yet to see estate agents' particulars describing either the site area in hectares, room sizes in metres or the floor area of the house in square metres.

MOVING IN

Once you accept that the building is complete, the contractor effectively hands the house over to you and it becomes your responsibility, so do make sure that you have it properly insured. There are bound to be one or two teething problems; remember, every house is a prototype, unlike the family saloon. Use your discretion as to when to summon the builder.

For a period of six months, under the terms of the contract, you retain 2.5 per cent of the final contract sum over what is called the 'defects liability period'. Usually, the problems relate to movement and shrinkage as a result of the building 'drying out'. Cracks may appear and doors may not close properly which should not be the result of major structural problems, and it is fair to keep a list so that the contractor can return at the end of six months to rectify these items. Your architect will normally carry out an inspection at this stage so that all the matters can be attended to, and once complete a final certificate issued. The final payment must now be made.

With luck you will then be left in peace to enjoy your own individual home.

C H A P T E R 6

BUILDING YOUR OWN HOUSE AND THE LAW

WAYNE THOMAS

Wayne Thomas is a partner with solicitors Holt and Sellars, of Worcester, where he specialises in the acquisition of plots for self-builders.

Buying a building plot in England and Wales is not the same as buying a house. Many more legal questions need to be considered and, if these are ignored, your self-build project will be at risk.

The solicitor plays an essential role in ensuring that your plans become a reality and that you will not incur any unforeseen expenses. This is a specialist area; before instructing a firm of solicitors you should satisfy yourself that they have plenty of experience in acting for individual buyers of building plots.

If you are building your own home, the work carried out by the solicitor will be divided into two broad categories:

- The first is to transfer the legal title of the building plot into your name with the assurance that there are no restrictions affecting the title which would prevent it being built upon.

- The second is to ensure that your home can be built in accordance with your wishes and within your planned budget. This will involve a number of practical considerations, including the availability of services, conditions of planning permission and the provisions of any building contract.

BUYING YOUR PLOT

The legal procedure

Whenever you initially agree to buy a building plot, the agreement is stated to be 'subject to contract'. This means that you have not legally committed yourself to the purchase and can withdraw if you find there are problems. Having agreed to buy your building plot 'subject to contract', you can instruct your solicitors to carry out the necessary work.

They will start by looking carefully at the contract which has been prepared by the vendor's solicitors. The contract sets out details of the land which is being sold and the price you have agreed. It also sets out the contractual relationship of the buyer and vendor and this is usually done by incorporating individual details into a standard form of Conditions of Sale approved by the Law Society.

These standard Conditions of Sale regulate the rights and obligations of the buyer and vendor once a binding contract has been entered into. The vendor's solicitors will advise whether they consider the amendments to the standard form to be acceptable.

The contract for a building plot sale will usually contain some additional provisions, particularly if the vendor is retaining some adjoining land. For example, the vendor may reserve rights for pipes, wires and cables to cross the building plot. You may also be granted similar rights over the vendor's retained land. In addition, there may be a number of restrictions regarding how the land is to be used or even what should be built on it.

If you are not happy with the contract, your solicitors will try to negotiate amendments which will be more acceptable to you. The success of such negotiations will depend to some degree on the demand for and supply of building plots in the area. If good building plots are in short supply and there are plenty of potential buyers, the vendor may adopt a 'take or leave it' attitude.

In a poor property market where there is a shortage of buyers who are actually in a position to proceed, your solicitors may be able to insist that the contract reflects your requirements. It is possible that no agreement can be reached, in which case you can withdraw from the transaction before it is too late.

Your solicitors will also study the legal title to the property. They will check that the vendor owns the building plot and also that no restrictions have been imposed in the past that would prevent you from building your home. Restrictions of this sort are known as 'restrictive covenants' and if you breach them you could face court action for damages or even an injunction ordering you not to build your home.

When checking the legal title, your solicitors will make sure that you have all necessary rights which ensure access to the plot and the connection of services such as drains, water supply and electricity cables. If the plot does not already benefit from such rights, the vendor must be able to show that he is entitled to grant them to you when you buy the plot.

The legal title will not reveal everything that your solicitors need to know about the building plot and it will be necessary for them to make further enquiries. Some enquiries will be of a practical nature and be directed to the vendor via his solicitors. Others will be standard form 'searches' and be directed to various organisations for specific information relating to the land itself or the area in which it is located.

Your solicitors will always make a local search which comprises a set of enquiries to the local authority. It will reveal local land charges affecting the property such as planning decisions, compulsory purchase orders, financial charges and tree preservation orders. The local search will also provide information on numerous other important matters such as public maintenance of highways and drains, smoke control orders, breaches of planning control and existence of public footpaths.

If the plot abuts a village green or common land, your solicitors will send a Commons Registration Search to the county council. This reveals whether any part of the plot of land is registered as common land which might be subject to rights that may be exercised by other people, such as the grazing of cattle, which would prevent any building on the plot. Also, if the plot is in an area in which coal mining takes place or has taken place in the past, your solicitor may send a Mining Search to British Coal. This will reveal the existence of any underground workings which may cause problems with subsidence.

At this stage your solicitors will inspect the planning permission relating to the building plot. They will ensure that it is valid and confirm the date upon which it will expire. Your attention will also be brought to any conditions in the planning permission which may affect your decision to proceed with the purchase.

Once this work has been completed, it will be safe for you to enter into a binding agreement for the purchase of the plot. This is assuming that you have finance available for buying the plot and building your home. If a mortgage is required, you should not commit yourself until a firm mortgage offer is received from a lending institution. In most cases, the mortgage offer will be subject to a number of conditions before the loan can be made. Your solicitors will make sure that all these conditions can be satisfied before you go any further.

A binding agreement is entered into by exchanging contracts. This is when the buyer signs a copy of the contract which is then sent to the vendor's solicitors together with a deposit, usually 10 per cent of the purchase price. The vendor also signs a contract which is then sent to the buyer's solicitors. Having exchanged contracts neither side can withdraw from the agreement except in exceptional circumstances where the other party has been in breach of contract. If as a buyer you try to back out at this stage you would be liable to lose your deposit.

On exchange of contracts a completion date is set, at which point the building plot will legally change hands and you will become the owner. The completion date could be only a few days after exchange of contracts, or it could be a number of months. It all depends on what you have agreed with the vendor. The solicitors on both sides deal with further formalities during the interval between exchange of contracts and completion, and when the day comes the balance of the purchase price is paid to the vendor's solicitors and the title deeds are handed over.

You are now the proud owner of a building plot.

Buying a plot at auction

If you bid for a plot at auction and are successful, you are deemed to have entered into a binding contract for its purchase. It does not matter whether it is legally or physically unsuitable for your proposed building. You are stuck with it.

It is, therefore, important that if you are interested in land that is coming up at auction you should inform your solicitors immediately. They will contact the vendor's solicitors for the contract documentation. Usually, a copy local search will be available. There may be sufficient time for your solicitors to make the necessary enquiries, but often this is not the case. It is also unlikely that you will have all the necessary surveys carried out on the off chance that your bid will be successful. Needless to say, it is necessary to have the finance sorted out before walking into the auction room. It is most unwise to commit yourself to the purchase and then look for a mortgage, particularly as you are likely to have to complete the transaction within 28 days.

The risks associated with buying a building plot at auction may be outweighed by picking up a 'bargain', but you should be wary. It is always worth putting in an offer, subject to contract, before the auction. This may be attractive to the vendor who may be worried that the same price will not be achieved if the auction goes ahead. If so, the plot may be withdrawn from the auction and you can proceed with the purchase in the normal way. Similarly, if a plot is not sold at auction because it has not reached its reserve price it may be worth approaching the vendor afterwards to agree a private sale.

LEGAL TITLE

It will already be appreciated how important it is for your solicitors to investigate the legal title to a building plot thoroughly before you commit yourself to purchasing it. They will be particularly concerned with the following:

Rights and easements

In some cases a building plot will abut a public road from which all services such as drains, water supply, gas pipes and electricity cables can be directly connected. Access to the plot will also be direct from the road and so there will be no need for rights of any sort to be granted over the adjoining land.

If your plot fits this description, consider yourself very lucky. Unfortunately, this is often not the case. By their very nature, individual building plots are frequently 'back land' development at the rear of existing houses.

There may be two or more building plots together which will need to share a means of access as well as other facilities. In such cases the plots must be granted certain legal rights or easements.

Of prime importance is full vehicular access to the plot. If there is no direct access from a public road there must be a right of way granted over the adjoining land which permits vehicle access at all times and for all purposes. This right must benefit not only you but also anyone visiting the plot with your authority and, of course, any future owners of the plot. You should also ensure that there will be no difficulty in construction vehicles using it during the building of your home.

Equally, if your pipes, wires and cables need to go under other people's land before connection to the mains, further rights will have to be granted over their land. For example, you will need the right for water, gas and electricity to pass under their property as well as the right to enter it in order to lay the services and maintain them in the future.

If you intend to build right up to the boundary with the adjoining land you will need a right of entry in order to maintain the outside wall. A similar situation applies if you are responsible for the upkeep or maintenance of a boundary wall or hedge.

Shared facilities

Where a building plot comprises part of the garden of another property, it is often desirable to connect into the pipes, wires and cables which already serve the existing property. Similarly, if it forms part of a multi-plot development, the various plots are likely to share services as well as an access road.

The appropriate rights and easements will have to be granted. However, there is one further complication which needs to be considered, because at some stage in the future the shared facilities will need to be repaired and maintained. The question then arises as to who should carry out this work and whether anyone else should contribute to the cost.

These matters must be dealt with and your solicitors will be particularly concerned with the detailed wording of the rights and obligations. For example, it is common to indicate that you will pay a 'fair proportion' of the cost of such maintenance and repair. But who decides what is fair? A dispute could result in costly and time-consuming court proceedings unless your solicitors insist upon such disputes being subject to arbitration.

One way of avoiding uncertainty of this sort is to agree that you will be responsible for a set proportion of repair and maintenance costs, but even this can have its dangers if future development takes place which involves the use of the shared facilities by additional properties.

Restrictive covenants

You may own the freehold of your building plot and you may have planning permission to build your dream home on it. But if the land is affected by a restrictive covenant you may not be able to lay a single brick.

If the vendor of land wishes to restrict or have some control over the future use of that land, he can impose a covenant on the buyer. This amounts to a promise by the buyer to abide by the vendor's requirements and it will remain equally binding for any future buyers of the land.

For example, there may be restrictions which limit the number of houses that can be built on a certain area of land and the construction of your house could result in this limit being exceeded. If so, the person having the benefit of the covenant would be able to obtain a court injunction preventing you from building at all.

Quite often, fresh restrictive covenants are imposed by vendors of plots who intend to continue living on the adjoining land. They will naturally wish to maintain their quality of life and ensure that the new building will have a minimum effect on the value of their retained land. Typical examples of such restrictions are:

- to use the new property for the occupation of one family only
- not to use the new property in connection with any business, trade or profession
- not to do or permit anything which may be a nuisance or annoyance to the property retained by the vendor

- to fence and thereafter maintain the new boundary between the building plot and the vendor's retained land
- not to fell certain mature trees on the plot without the vendor's consent
- not to construct your home or carry out any extensions or structural alterations in the future without first obtaining the vendor's approval.

The last of these covenants is particularly important and your solicitors are likely to advise that it should only be accepted if there is a proviso that such consent shall not be unreasonably refused. If building plans exist or detailed planning permission has been obtained prior to the exchange of contracts, the vendor's approval can be obtained at that stage and incorporated in the contract.

It should be remembered that covenants can also be imposed on a vendor by a buyer and this is important when the vendor is retaining the adjoining land. Having invested a good deal of time and money in buying your plot and building your home, you will not wish your enjoyment to be adversely affected by the unsympathetic use or development of the vendor's retained land.

You may be particularly concerned that the vendor does not erect further buildings on the retained land without your consent, since they may well overlook your new home. Equally, you are likely to be anxious that the retained land should only be used for residential purposes and not be converted to commercial use.

If you gain access to your plot by a right of way over the retained land, you will want to ensure that the right of way is never obstructed by the vendor.

In each case your interests can be protected by requiring the vendor to enter into the appropriate covenants. These will vary from one plot to another but your solicitors will advise which covenants should be requested in your particular case.

Ransoms

Mention has already been made of the consequences of being in breach of a restrictive covenant. You may be sued for damages or prevented from building altogether. Alternatively, the person who has the benefit of the covenant may be prepared to release your land from it – at a price. This is a typical ransom which must be guarded against when buying a building plot.

If you find yourself held to ransom it will be necessary to allocate substantial funds in order to pay the ransom and, if you are working to a tight budget, it may threaten the feasibility of the whole project. Your solicitors will, therefore, be attempting to ensure that this does not happen.

Ransoms can come about in a number of ways. One is where there is a restriction on the number of houses that can be built on a particular area of land. For example, when a council house is sold to a tenant the local authority usually insists that the buyer enters into a covenant only to use the land as a single dwelling. If the buyer subsequently decides to use part of the garden as a building plot, it will not be possible to build on the plot unless the local authority agrees to release the land from the covenant. It is unlikely to do this without payment of a substantial sum.

Access to the plot can also give rise to a ransom. For example, the building plot may be very close to a public road but may be separated from the road by a narrow strip of land. There should be no problems provided the appropriate right of access is granted by the vendor. However, if the strip of land is owned by someone else, they can prevent you from gaining access unless a ransom is paid.

Your solicitors will examine any deed plans to ensure that the front boundary of the plot is co-extensive with the road or footpath abutting it. If this is a public road, there should be no question of a ransom strip arising. By way of precaution, your solicitors may obtain a letter from the highway authority confirming that the building plot does indeed abut highway land.

Unfortunately, deed plans can sometimes be inaccurate or even misleading. It is, therefore, important that you should inspect the site itself very carefully. The position of the front boundary should be checked and you should be on your guard if it is marked by a wall, fence or hedge which is separated from the road by a strip of land or green verge.

Ransoms can also arise where the building plot is affected by easements where the owners of adjoining property have rights over the land. If the building of your home affects these rights in any way you may be prevented from carrying out the work and once again be held to ransom. A simple example is where neighbouring land drains into a septic tank on the building plot which would have to be repositioned before any building took place. This could not be done without the neighbour's permission and such permission may only be given upon payment of a ransom.

Easements of this sort are usually apparent from the title deeds and your solicitors will make you fully aware of them. However, some of these easements may have been created many years ago and may be obsolete. Other rights may have been acquired by long use and not feature in the title deeds. It is, therefore, always advisable to inspect the site carefully to see if any rights are actually being exercised.

Indemnity policies

You can only be held to ransom if the owner of a ransom strip, or the person with the benefit of a restrictive covenant, can be contacted. But what if your solicitor is unable to trace them? This is not as unlikely as it sounds, particularly where the person who has the benefit of the covenant or ransom strip no longer lives in the locality.

You are then left in a dilemma. You know that the covenant or ransom strip exists, but you do not know who to contact to resolve the problem. It is possible that you could go ahead and never be troubled in the future. But it is equally possible that at some time in the future the person benefiting from the covenant or ransom strip may turn up and make a claim against you. Even if this does not happen, you may have difficulty in selling the property at a later stage if you do not have protection against this sort of eventuality.

Protection can usually be obtained in the form of an indemnity policy with an insurance company. This covers you for losses arising from such a claim being made against the property in the future. It is important to ensure that the indemnity policy provides sufficient cover should a claim be made and over the years it may be necessary to increase the amount of cover.

The cost of obtaining an indemnity policy varies according to the circumstances. As with any insurance policy, the premium will be calculated according to the amount of cover required and the likelihood of a claim being made.

(*Continued on page 105.*)

THE LEGEND
BRINGS VERSATILITY TO LIFE

With a timeless, classical beauty, the Legend gas fire from Main provides a versatile and attractive focal point – a place to sit and dream.

At home in any decor, traditional or modern, its realistic flame picture is produced by a combination of burners to give a cosy warm glow and lively, dancing flames.

Simple to control, the Legend produces a maximum heat output of 4 kW, enough to heat most living rooms whatever the weather outside.

Available as a free standing fire, the Legend can also be combined with a back boiler from the Potterton Myson Housewarmer range to provide whole house central heating and domestic hot water, or with a Main Carina E back circulator to supply hot water for all your household needs.

Elegantly attractive, the Legend really does bring versatility to life.

POTTERTON MYSON
PART OF BLUE CIRCLE

WE MEAN BUSINESS

FOR FURTHER INFORMATION PLEASE CONTACT SALES OFFICE.
POTTERTON MYSON, EASTERN AVENUE. TEAM VALLEY TRADING ESTATE. GATESHEAD. TYNE & WEAR. NE11 0PG.
TEL: 091 491 4466. FAX: 091 491 7568

POTTERTON MYSON
PART OF BLUE CIRCLE

A LIVING LEGEND FROM POTTERTON MYSON

When Potterton Myson launched the Main Legend in the summer of 1992, it marked the re-branding of Main Gas to 'Main' within the extensive company stable of domestic heating appliances. The Legend was the first fire to carry the new logo featuring the Main name topped by the distinctive Blue Circle arc.

The famous Blue Circle arc is testament to the fact that Potterton Myson is part of Blue Circle Industries and the UK's largest manufacturer of domestic heating appliances for the home.

The Main Legend, a live fuel effect fire is one of the company's more recent gas fire innovations. The Legend is a classic blend of traditional styling and realistic living flames with glowing coals, and was launched only after extensive research to determine exactly what consumers were looking for.

The Legend blends with both traditional and modern decor; its solid 'cast iron' appearance belies the Legend's light weight. The aluminium casing provides a light, compact fire which fits easily onto 12in. hearths and most fire surrounds.

From the solid cast canopy to the cast fender with fretted grilles and brass finials, every inch of the Legend spells craftsmanship and quality. The casing has discreet brass-finish trims and the 'realistic-effect' flickering flame and glowing coals provide the perfect winter focal point of any home.

The fuel bed itself comprises of hard ceramic coals on a moulded ceramic base, with location pegs and numbers for simple and accurate arrangement.

These and other design features of the Legend were incorporated as a direct result of consumer research. Susan Conroy is Product Manager with responsibility for the Legend and says, "Today's consumers are not simply looking for a high performance fire; they also want an attractive focal point in their living room."

Research and development throughout this period has led to many changes, including new burner technology, improved long life hard ceramic coals and updates in fire design. In particular, consumers can now enjoy the benefits of realistic coal beds with flickering flames, canopy finishes, convector grilles and fender finish.

With four heat settings controlling more than 4kW of heat, the Legend's combination of convected warmth from the canopy grille and radiant heat from the live coal effect firebed will provide comfortable surroundings, whatever the weather. An integral piezo spark and flame supervision device provides complete control and security.

The Legend is also available as a firefront for the Housewarmer backboiler, although both the fire and backboiler do operate independently. The Housewarmer backboiler is powerful enough to provide full central heating for the whole house; in the summer months independent operation provides a plentiful supply of hot water.

Although the backboiler market in the UK has remained fairly static in recent years, it still accounts for around 20% of the total market. The backboiler, like the Housewarmer, is seen by many installers and consumers as an ideal way of providing hot water and heating for the modern home being economical, controllable and saves on living space.

Ease of fitting in particular is a key feature of the Housewarmer range of backboilers. The backboiler is designed to simply slide into the fireplace opening and its connections result in a straightforward installation.

The Housewarmer backboiler is available in two outputs – 45,000Btu/h and 55,000Btu/h. Both incorporate the efficiency of cast iron and both work independently of the fire when necessary.

Consumers and installers know that when they invest in a Main gas fire they also invest in the peace of mind that only the UK's largest heating manufacturer can bring. The company's support service operation is second to none, with over 80 fully trained engineers in the field.

The Technical Helpline – which is manned full time by up to a dozen personnel who are all experts on the Potterton Myson gas fire range – means that in the unlikely event of needing help, instant and on-the-spot advice is a simple call away. The Helpline can make available information on all Potterton Myson products and their use in heating systems.

Also designed to minimise the inconvenience for householders is the extensive parts operation to ensure Potterton Myson products are back in full service in the shortest possible time. There is currently a nationwide network of Interpart stockists which can supply parts for products both new and old. This is backed up by Curzon which operates an 11 outlet, computer linked parts and supply service.

If you would like to receive further information on the Legend and Housewarmer, call Potterton Myson's Brochure Hotline free on telephone number 0800 665533.

It should be mentioned that there is a procedure whereby covenants can be set aside by an application to the Lands Tribunal. However, the procedure is a lengthy one and can incur considerable costs. As with most court proceedings, the outcome can never be certain and so you are unlikely to be advised to adopt this course of action if it is possible to obtain an indemnity policy.

BUILDING YOUR HOME: PRACTICAL CONSIDERATIONS WITH LEGAL IMPLICATIONS

In dealing with the purchase of your building plot, your solicitors are mainly concerned to ensure that there is no legal reason why a house should not be built on it and for that house to have the benefit of the necessary right of access and the provision of services. But there is more to it than this. You probably want a specific type of house, in a specific position on the site, which is to be built within a specific budget.

To avoid disappointment, there are other practical considerations which need to be taken into account and which your solicitors will bring to your attention.

Boundaries

It is not only to avoid tripping over ransom strips that the exact boundaries of your building plot have to be established.

Most importantly, you will want to ensure that, having purchased the plot, you will not become involved in any dispute relating to either the position or the ownership of the boundaries. The likelihood of such disputes arising on the sale of a building plot is higher than in the case of a ready-made house, simply because in many cases the plot sale involves the creation of at least one new boundary.

It is always recommended that, prior to exchanging contracts on a plot purchase, there should be a physical walking of boundaries, preferably in the company of a surveyor, who will be able to point out any possible future sources of dispute. If the position of the boundaries is not self-evident, your solicitors will request the vendor to have them physically pegged out.

This will be needed if the vendor is retaining some adjoining land, or where the plot forms part of a large development. Your solicitors are also likely to request that there be added to the contract for the sale of the plot a clause confirming that the pegged boundaries shall prevail in the event of any discrepancy with the contract plan.

Depending on the individual circumstances, your solicitors may also recommend that the plot be measured and the dimensions be included in the contract plan. In this way, it is unlikely that there will be disputes at any time in the future as to the position of the boundaries. Taking measurements may also be helpful when dealing with the planners, particularly if there are any critical distances involved, such as the length of the rear garden or the minimum distance between habitable rooms.

Having established the position of the boundaries, it may be important to find out who actually owns them, since this will have a bearing on the erection and future maintenance of fences, walls or hedges.

In the case of a new boundary between your plot and the vendor's retained land, this should be dealt with in the contract for the sale of the plot. In other cases, where boundaries abut the land of third parties, the necessary information may be included in the title deeds. However, if the deeds are silent it may be necessary for your solicitors to contact the owners of the adjoining land in an attempt to clarify the situation.

Ground conditions

Although there may be no legal reason why your plot should not be purchased and built upon, it does not mean that you can rush into the exchange of contracts. The suitability of that land for building needs to be established, otherwise you may find that the plot can only be built upon if a considerable amount is spent in making it suitable.

Your solicitor will emphasise the importance of making all possible enquiries as to past uses of the land. If it is former industrial land, or perhaps the site of an old petrol station, it could have been contaminated by the deposit of noxious materials. Alternatively, the site may have been used for tipping rubbish and thus necessitate special foundations.

Although enquiries may reveal a certain amount about the suitability of the site, this is not a substitute for having proper surveys carried out. Many self-builders disregard their solicitors' advice to do this in the mistaken belief that if there are existing houses nearby, there should be no problem in building on the plot. This is not the case and if you proceed with the purchase without having surveys, you are taking a risk.

If the site is properly surveyed you will receive full details of the soil conditions which will enable the type of foundations which may be required by the building inspector or the National House-Building Council (NHBC) to be established.

The survey will also reveal whether the building will have to be protected from any adjoining hedges or trees by root barriers. You will also need to know about any geological problems which could result in land slippage or subsidence. If there are any existing ponds, ditches, streams or marshland, they may require diverting, draining or culverting, which would again add to the cost of the project. The same applies if there are existing on-site wells or if there is an existing building which needs to be demolished and which has a cellar. The survey should also draw to your attention the need for any additional works, such as the erection of retaining walls.

Finally, you will need to be advised as to the suitability of the site for drainage. If it is intended to connect the foul drain to the council sewer, the position of the plot must be such that there is a suitable fall. If not, you will have to take into account the additional cost of a pump system. If it is not intended to connect into the mains, the survey will deal with the suitability of the soil where it is proposed to employ a biodisc treatment plant or septic tank, together with the adequacy of the land for a feather drain run-off and any soak-away system.

Having agreed to purchase your plot 'subject to contract', it is important that you have the survey carried out as soon as possible. Good building plots are in short supply and there is likely to be pressure to exchange contracts at an early date. But it is no good exchanging contracts and committing yourself to the purchase only to find out subsequently that to build on the site will be prohibitively expensive.

Services

It is essential in any self-build project that the house will receive all the essential services. For this reason, a great deal of emphasis has already been placed on the need to ensure that the plot has the benefit of all the necessary rights and easements (see pages 95–105).

There is also the practical consideration of exactly how the connections can be made. Your solicitors will normally write to the appropriate authorities with a plan of the site, enquiring as to the route of the mains and as to whether there will be any problem in making a connection. This is particularly important with foul drainage, since it may be necessary to connect into a private drainage run before it in turn connects with the mains.

Not only will you need the right to connect into the private run, and to bear the cost of the possible ransom that might entail, but it will also be necessary to check the condition and capacity of the private run. Otherwise, you could find yourself contributing to unexpected repair and maintenance costs in the future.

When making enquiries regarding the availability of connections to the mains, your solicitors will also check that no existing services cross the site.

If they do, it may prevent building altogether. Alternatively, it may be possible to proceed after diverting the existing services. The feasibility of doing this must be investigated before you commit yourself to the purchase.

Planning

The vast majority of building plots are offered for sale with the benefit of 'outline' planning permission (see pages 79–80). This means that permission has been granted for the erection of a house, but no building can take place until fuller details are approved by the local authority.

In most cases the outline planning permission will have a number of conditions attached to it which will give you some guidance as to the type of detailed plans that are likely to be approved. These conditions may deal with such things as the size of the proposed house, the number of permitted storeys, the removal of mature trees and access to the site.

Your solicitor will usually receive a copy of the outline planning permission along with the contract documentation shortly after the plot purchase has been initially agreed, subject to contract. They will be mainly concerned to ensure that the planning permission has not expired or is not going to expire in the near future. They will also take care to check that the conditions can be satisfied from a legal point of view.

For example, it is common for the outline planning permission to include a condition that the entry to the plot is constructed in such a way as to allow 'sight lines' or 'visibility splays'. Sometimes minimum dimensions are specified and it is important to ensure that they can be incorporated within the frontage of the building plot. If not, the planning permission could not be complied with unless you encroached upon your neighbour's land.

In this situation, you would have to buy the affected land or enter into a deed with the neighbour as to its future use. This would, of course, have to be done before you enter into a binding contract to purchase the plot. Otherwise, you could find yourself held to ransom.

Even if you and your solicitors are quite happy with the conditions imposed in the outline planning permission, it does not mean that you will necessarily be able to build the home that you have in mind. This will all depend upon getting detailed planning permission.

Ideally, this should be obtained before you exchange contracts on the purchase of the plot, but this is not always possible because the vendor may not be prepared to wait for such a long time before you commit yourself to the purchase. If there is another buyer interested in the plot, you could lose it.

In such cases, your solicitors are likely to recommend that your architect, or the design firm being used to draw up your plans, should meet the local planning officer at an early stage to discuss your proposals in principle. If it is clear at that stage that your plans will not fit in with the prerequisites or special requirements of the local authority, you can withdraw.

Alternatively, you can reconsider your proposals to make them comply with the special requirements.

Any additional plans will have to be drawn up to reflect any information that has been revealed by the local search obtained by your solicitors. For example, the local search may show that the land is subject to a tree preservation order or is in a conservation area which will involve the imposition of special building constraints.

Although you may be prepared to proceed to exchange of contracts on the basis of only an outline planning permission, there may still be obstacles if you require a mortgage to build the plot. In the wake of the slump in house prices of the last four years and the high level of repossessions, the lending institutions are extremely cautious when it comes to granting mortgages for self-build projects. It is now common for mortgage offers to be conditional upon full detailed planning permission being obtained.

This creates a problem if the vendor is pushing hard for a binding exchange of contracts on the basis that the land already has outline planning permission. You cannot commit yourself to the purchase without being guaranteed the mortgage money, but this cannot be guaranteed until you have the detailed planning permission.

Your solicitors may be able to resolve the dilemma by negotiating an exchange of contracts conditional upon a satisfactory detailed planning consent and mortgage offer being obtained. However, the wording of such a contract needs to be very carefully considered.

CONSTRUCTION

Building contracts

Some self-builders intend to carry out some or most of the building work themselves. Others have a substantial amount of work carried out by subcontractors on their behalf, but a large proportion of the self-build market is made up of people who want an individual home which is suited to their specific requirements but which they intend to have built entirely by an independent contractor.

In such cases, it is essential that you have a building contract that incorporates a detailed specification of both what will be built and the materials which are to be used. It should also contain provisions which protect you from defective workmanship, unavailability of materials or failure to keep within agreed time-limits.

The building contract should also incorporate procedures dealing with variation of the original specification, payment for work done, insurance of the works and termination of the agreement. Many builders have a standard form of contract which deals adequately with such matters, but you would be well advised to have it checked by your solicitors to ensure that you are properly protected.

If you have employed an architect to design your home, he might also be retained as the supervising officer to ensure that each stage of construction is completed in accordance with his requirements. If the builder does not have a suitable form of standard building contract, you may wish to suggest the JCT Agreement for Minor Building Works which is produced by the Joint Contracts Tribunal (see page 86). This incorporates the necessary clauses and also provides for the appointment of a supervising officer.

Even though it is in a standard form, it should still be examined by your solicitors since some amendment might be required to suit your requirements. For example, you may be using a mortgage to finance the construction of the house. If so, the mortgage offer will specify how many stage payments will be made by the lender, as well as the stages of construction that must be reached for such payments to be receivable. The builder will also want payment in stages and it is important to ensure that the provisions in the building contract are compatible with the mortgage offer.

Guarantees

To ensure that the new house has been properly constucted, it should be covered by the appropriate NHBC, or Architect's Certificate. One of these is usually required for mortgage purposes and without them you would find it very difficult to sell your home in the future.

NHBC Certificate

The National House-Building Council provides a scheme under which houses are designed and built to a set of standards by builders on its register. In the first two years after the house has been built the builder is obliged to remedy any defect which results from a breach of NHBC's technical requirements. If the builders fail to do this, the NHBC will make good any resulting loss.

In addition, the NHBC will cover any loss resulting from defects or major damage to the structure resulting from settlement subsidence or heave. Damage to the drainage system is also covered. This aspect of the NHBC guarantee applies from the third to the tenth year after the house has been built.

If your home is being constructed by an NHBC registered builder, your solicitors will ensure that they receive the NHBC Buildmark Book and Ten Year Notice upon completion of the build. These will be forwarded to you and should then be kept safe.

Architect's Certificate

In the absence of an NHBC certificate you would need an Architect's Certificate confirming that the architect has inspected the building at each stage of construction and that it complies with the given specification. Should any problems occur in the future, legal action can be taken against the architect.

The Architect's Certificate will be placed with the title deeds, and at the same time disclosure should be obtained of the architect's professional indemnity insurance to ensure enforceability of the professional duty of care.

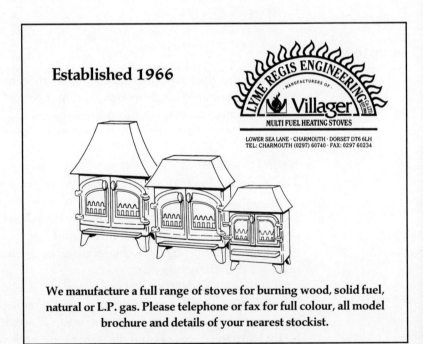

CHAPTER

DESIGNING AND INSTALLING KITCHENS AND BATHROOMS

TOM ROWLAND

KITCHENS

The kitchen is one of the most important rooms in the house, whether because as a family you tend to congregate there, or because you do a lot of entertaining and need a functional room in which to cook elaborate meals. Building on an individual basis gives you the opportunity to think ahead – unlike an off-the-peg house.

Before you start you need to think carefully about what you want from your kitchen, and it is a good idea to allocate more space to it in your house plans than you think you will need. It is easy to use the surplus by adding furniture or work tops, not so easy to change the room size once your house is built. It is also worth doing sketches and spending time talking to your builder/architect/kitchen designer about your lifestyle.

This means that you need to decide if the end product is to be principally a family room where you will spend a great deal of time with your children or your friends, or a gourmet meal production line.

If the family comes first, think about a children's area, where they can play safely without getting under your feet while you are cooking, and about creating a warm, friendly atmosphere. You also need to decide if you want a joint kitchen/dining room where you can do most of your entertaining.

If the kitchen is going to be more like the headquarters of an attempt at a gourmet cook of the year competition than the preparation area for fish fingers and beans, and you intend to do a lot of formal entertaining, it is worth considering a separate dining area which is clearly visible from the kitchen. There are many units available now which are effective at creating an area 'beyond the kitchen' for this purpose.

If the kitchen is mainly a place to prepare breakfast and children's meals, perhaps you need just a breakfast bar.

A separate laundry/utility room

If space allows, and you have a large family, a separate utility room is a huge boon, especially if you intend to use the kitchen as a family room/dining room. Having the washing whizzing around is not conducive to eating a civilized evening meal.

Here, and in the kitchen proper, there are several basic planning rules which must be followed – and which any experienced kitchen planner will know about. This is doubly important when there are children or elderly family members to consider. There should always be plenty of work-top space next to the oven – with a heat-proof ceramic counter saver on it – on which to rest hot dishes. It should not be necessary to cross the kitchen to take hot pans from the hob to the sink for draining.

Lockable cabinets are available which can be fitted inside units to store medicines and potentially harmful household cleaners (bleach, etc). And there are simple magnetic door catches for all base unit doors.

'The look'

This is not so much a question of cost as personal taste, and you can be as adventurous as you like. Most 'looks' are affordable if you shop around.

Certainly, the days when the colour of most kitchen units could correctly be described as 'porridge' are long gone. Nowadays there is a variety of styles to choose from. But it is probably as well to stick to one school of design, even if you mix elements.

- High-tec, with high-gloss laminates and lots of fully fitted units with a place for everything. Lots of chrome/stainless steel/black and white.
- Country-style in warm solid wood. There is a choice now of oak, beech and alder, as well as pine. The end product has lots of niches and plate racks, open shelves and probably a decorative cornice.
- Cheerful, coloured kitchen; there is plenty of red, blue, turquoise – even lilac – to choose from.
- A painted kitchen; units hand finished to a design and colours especially for you.
- And a theme prevalent today – 'the unfitted kitchen'. If you're tired of the totally streamlined look, but recognise the need for lots of storage to avoid a messy kitchen, take a look at the options now available for choosing individual units which fit together where you want them to, but which can also be used individually, taking in dressers, storage cupboards, larders, wine racks.

How to spend your budget sensibly

Essentially, you get what you pay for. Quality kitchen units are exactly that; the quality of materials and construction are reflected in the price. Virtually all mass-produced carcasses are made from chipboard which is a stable material. But there are many different grades of chipboard. The top grade is E1, an environmentally friendly chipboard, now used by many of the leading German manufacturers. Cheaper grade chipboard has a softer inner core, and will not therefore stand up to as much hard wear as the higher grades.

You can have a wood carcass, but this is going to cost a lot more money without necessarily being any more serviceable than a high-grade chipboard.

As a general rule, top quality units are 600mm deep; some cheaper units are only 500mm, which will affect kitchen planning since work tops will have to be deeper to take built-in appliances (all 600mm deep).

Some work tops are only 30mm thick; but all quality work tops are 40mm thick, giving much greater stability.

Quality of construction is important; the stability of units is vital. Ask how the units you think you would like are constructed.

Flat-pack kitchens may be cheaper to buy. But check on the additional fitting costs that may be involved; the units have to be assembled on site and, unless you can do this yourself, fitting charges can escalate.

Sinks and taps

Perhaps the best advice here is to spend time thinking about your sink and taps. They are all too often the last things to be considered, with the decision often involving the cheapest to be found, since most of the budget has already been spent on units and appliances.

In the long term this is bad planning. If you think of the time spent at the kitchen sink (research has shown that, in 87 per cent of British homes, someone is working at the sink for 288 hours a year), it is easy to see that choosing badly will be a daily source of aggravation, so it is well worth spending time researching the options available.

Choosing what your sink is made of is also an important decision. There are different grades of stainless steel, and it pays to go for quality. If you want a coloured sink, check on the material and finish. There have been problems with some synthetic sinks (some materials are difficult to clean, some are subject to thermal shock – the sink may crack under extremes of temperature). There are several quality synthetic materials; they are more expensive but they will not cause problems.

Decide whether you want two bowls; a drainer or two drainers; or one large bowl and a mobile drainer which you can store away, giving you more work-top space.

Then there are the taps which are enormously expensive. I have friends who have talked of throwing up promising careers in the professions because they are tempted by what seem huge profits to be made out of selling taps.

A good set can cost a third of the price of the boiler heating the water which flows through them, although nobody seems able to explain why the economies of scale which bring down the prices of other mass-engineered products do not apply to taps, even in big discount stores.

Apart from pure aesthetics *vis-à-vis* single-lever, cruciform, pillar taps, etc, there may be serious considerations if, for example, you are arthritic, in which case a single-lever tap which can be operated by the elbow is a sensible choice, while for the short person or wheelchair-bound a pull-out tap with a spray head makes washing up, cleaning fruit and vegetables or filling buckets and tall vases much easier.

Britain's fluctuating water pressures (they vary tremendously in different parts of the country or even in different parts of a neighbourhood) can cause problems. So if you want a single-lever tap or a pull-out spray tap, make sure that it has been designed to cope with the pressure conditions in your area.

Temperature control is important for safety. Check that your tap has good control, and check on the after-sales service offered by your supplier. If something goes wrong with a tap, you need immediate action.

Cooking appliances

How serious a cook are you? Even if you don't intend to cook a Sunday roast each week, don't necessarily choose the smallest oven. There will inevitably be times when you do want to cook more elaborately. Christmas can seem surprisingly frequent if, as you fail to fit all your roasting tins in at once, you are reminded that you made the wrong choice of oven. The choice between gas and electric is usually based on personal experience, though the convenience gap has narrowed now that fan-assisted electric ovens are almost as quick to pre-heat as gas. Decide which suits you best.

Oven door temperatures are a consideration. Check with the manufacturer about the maximum temperature that the outside of the door will reach during cooking. This is especially important when there are children around.

Pyrolytic cleaning is available on many models. The oven is heated to a high temperature for several hours and literally 'burns off' the grease. You just empty out the ashes at the end. This is convenient, and on an efficient oven the cost of electricity will be less than the cost of a can of oven cleaner.

With regard to hobs, there is a choice of gas, sealed plate electric, ceramic, ceramic with halogen, and lastly induction. This is the latest to be introduced and the makers claim that it combines the advantages of a wipe-clean ceramic hob with the speed of gas.

Microwaves come in a wide range from simple ones to combination machines with a grill and oven combined. Make sure that you buy one which will be large enough for your needs.

Laundry appliances

Check your water consumption carefully as all new homes could eventually have water meters. This also affects electricity costs as the more water that is used, the more there is to be heated. As a general rule, the cold-fill machines are cheaper to run.

Check the programme selections – some machines have good 'hand wash' options and shorter programmes for lightly soiled clothes.

Check the noise factor, especially if the washing machine is going into the kitchen.

For family homes, a full-size tumble dryer will be more useful than a washer/dryer, as one load can be drying while another is washing. Gas tumble dryers are now available and efficient to run.

Dishwashers

This is a luxury you can afford. Quality modern dishwashers now use around half the water and electricity it takes to wash up the equivalent load by hand. But do check consumption values before you buy. Some models are now safe with fine china.

Refrigeration

Again energy efficiency must be a high priority. The energy consumption of fridges and freezers cannot be reduced by using them less often. They are switched on 24 hours a day, 365 days a year.

If you are buying a fridge/freezer, look for a double compressor so that one section can be switched off independently.

Zoned appliances are now available with a compartment for storing meat.

CFC free appliances are also widely available. There is no direct benefit to the user but many manufacturers have not increased prices on these models, so choose them if you can.

No-frost refrigeration saves defrosting – the fridge defrosts automatically.

Refrigerated wine storage appliances can be bought from a handful of suppliers. For the wine buff, this is much cheaper than building a wine cellar.

BATHROOMS

When planning a bathroom, remember that you need a working area of activity space around each item of sanitary ware. It is no use cramming a small bathroom with all the latest designs if there isn't enough room to use them comfortably. You need to stand back from the washbasin when you bend over to wash your face; you need knee room either side of the WC; you might need to kneel in front of the bath to wash a baby, and so on.

Once you are happy with the overall plan and are sure that it will suit your family requirements, call in the plumber. He will be able to tell you what can (and cannot) be done and give you a written quotation (obtain more than one). Then start scheming; choosing colours; deciding on designs and ordering equipment.

It is often possible to create an illusion of space and elegance with decor and lighting effects; warm it up with cosy colours; cool it down with soft pastels; select stylish surfaces to co-ordinate or contrast in colour; add finishing touches with decorations and mirrors. And don't overlook ventilation – it is important to keep the steam at bay. You can imprint your bathroom with your own style; you can make it a room for relaxation or stimulation but, above all, make it a room for enjoyment!

The British Bathroom Council produces a helpful booklet on the 'where' and 'how' of bathroom layout and makes the planning stage as painless as possible. 'Room for Improvement' is full of ideas and practical tips on how to create additional bathroom space to your best advantage.

Tips for planning a new bathroom

Planning bathroom facilities which will be flexible as your family needs change takes careful forethought; often a spare bedroom can be converted or perhaps a large bathroom can be split in two.

The British Bathroom Council advises that it may be useful to focus your ideas along basic lines which follow the pattern of simple arithmetic: multiply; subtract; add; divide.

Multiply. Make more rooms from a big one. Can a spare bedroom be converted to incorporate an *en suite* facility? Could you use part of a large upstairs landing? Multiply your options by replacing a dressing table with a built-in vanity unit or fit a shower cubicle into a run of wardrobe cupboards.

Subtract. Take away a wall and you gain both space and greater scope for a better bathroom. Perhaps a rather Spartan single WC and separate bathroom can be united to provide one luxurious room with the addition of two washbasins and a bidet. You can sometimes do this because the 'activity space' that must surround each item of bathroom equipment can be allowed to overlap.

Add. Adding to the number of separate bathroom facilities in your home helps to spread the load more widely, especially in the morning 'rush hour'. Think about the benefits of having a vanity unit in the bedroom. Consider transforming a walk-in cupboard into a cloakroom with WC and hand-rinse basin, or perhaps improving a cloakroom by adding a shower unit.

Divide. Sometimes dividing a large bathroom to give a separate WC provides a solution to the frustrating queue during the 'rush hour'. Space can be recovered by rehanging a door to open outwards if necessary.

Make a shopping list of the things you want in your new bathroom. What kind of bath (whirlpool, double, single, corner, fine acrylic or pressed steel)? What kind of shower (inside the bath or in a separate shower cubicle)? What kind of WC (close coupled cistern, high- or low-level cistern or a system with the cistern inset behind ducting in the wall)? What kind of washbasin (corner handbasin, cloakroom basin or deep wide basin)? And will you have a bidet?

Take careful measurements of the room. Then compare these with the sizes and shapes available in bathroom fittings and furniture. Draw a plan of the room on graph paper. Use cut-outs of bath, basin, WC, and so on, and move them around to get the best effect with optimum space. You may find, for example, that the WC is best moved to a separate location entirely. Remember, however, that the location of existing plumbing and soil pipe may limit your options.

Next, choose the colour. Current colours range from dark through pastel to white with options for added motifs. Often there are matching accessories.

Before installing your suite, discuss your plans with a qualified plumber. If you are building a bathroom extension you may need planning permission. Make sure that your new products and their installation comply with the water by-laws.

Obtain more than one fixed price quote from a qualified plumber. And ensure the quality and reliability of your new bathroom products by buying products made by a member of the British Bathroom Council.

Don't overlook ventilation and lighting when you 'upgrade' your bathroom. Removing steam with a window fan, for example, can make the bathroom much more pleasant, as well as removing the risk of mould growth or rot. Install spotlights or a make-up mirror with lights around the edge.

It is particularly important that any electrical work is carried out in accordance with current legislation – and that needs specialist advice. For advice on electrical work contact the National Inspection Council for Electrical Installation Contracting (NICEIC).

Baths

Acrylic

Acrylic baths are beautiful – they come in scores of shapes, sizes, styles and colours. They are smooth and glossy, warm to the touch and therefore pleasant to use.

They are made by heating 5mm or 8mm sheeting which becomes pliable – rather like a sheet of rubber – then is vacuum-formed in a bath-shaped mould. After cooling, the bath is removed from the mould and trimmed. Most acrylic baths are reinforced by glass fibre with a chipboard base bonded to the underside to provide strength. A galvanised steel frame provides rigidity and stability under the rim and the base of the bath. The average weight of an acrylic bath is just 30lb and this lightness makes it easy to handle and install.

The downside is that they can feel like plastic and the method of construction means that they have to be boxed in. Bathroom fittings are fashion products and the sorts of acrylic bath fitted in vast numbers in the 1960s and 1970s are now out of fashion.

Steel

Steel baths are incredibly hard-wearing. The thickness of steel used to make a steel bath varies from 1.5mm to 3mm. The thicker the steel, the stronger it is and the more resistant to damage. The steel is covered with porcelain or vitreous enamel which is chemical-, abrasion- and heat-resistant.

Steel baths are rust-proofed by chemically bonding a ground coat of black enamel which gives lifelong rust protection. The top coat of enamel can be virtually any colour, according to choice.

A steel bath usually has a roll-over rim to give smooth edges, and there is often a slip-resistant finish for extra safety.

All in a whirlpool

According to the trade, which obviously has a vested interest, these are the coming thing – the consumer durable that in a few years' time everybody who is anybody will have to have. Time will tell, but the individual home-builder has the option of being ahead of the trend because he has more flexibility in budgeting.

There are three basic types of whirlpool bath. There is no 'official' nomenclature and they are often referred to by the brand name of one of the first producers of whirlpools. But that's like calling all vacuum cleaners a Hoover. Generally speaking, a whirlpool bath recirculates water, a spa bath pumps air through the water in the bath and a whirlpool spa pumps a mixture of air and water.

The number and position of underwater jets can be varied, together with air and water pressure, to give a wide range of performance and control, including a pulsating cyclical action. Prices can be fairly modest for a basic system but, as with all things, you can pay a lot more if you want to.

Much has been written about the health-giving benefits of whirlpool spa baths. It is hard to quantify those benefits, but most people say that they feel better afterwards. The movement of water is supposed to provide a physical stimulus which, it is claimed, tones up muscles and eases away aches and pains. Perhaps it is best not to delve too deeply into hard facts – just relax and enjoy the experience.

But there are important aspects to choosing a whirlpool spa bath: quality of construction and performance, safety and hygiene. These qualities are being defined in new European standards currently being prepared, but they have not been formally published yet.

Which shower?

What are the differences between, and the benefits of, the different showers available?

Power showers
Low water pressure or low flow rate, common in many British homes, has led to a growing demand for showers which include a pump that automatically boosts the flow of hot and cold water supplies.

Power showers open up new areas of indulgence and satisfaction with the benefits of precise temperature control for comfort and safety. Adjustable heads are available to dispense a variety of spray formats – invigorating needle jets, a soft 'champagne foam' effect or an abundant waterfall shower.

You may need bigger hot and cold water storage tanks to supply the fairly high volume of water capable of being pumped through this type of shower. Your plumber should ensure that storage tanks can fill up as fast as they are emptied (because they can collapse if they do not).

A power shower can sometimes be fitted where other showers will not work. Even where the shower head is higher than the water storage tanks a special 'negative head' pump can be effective.

Don't forget that shower screens need to contain the increased spray associated with a power shower. Make sure that grouting between tiles and the seal around the edge of the shower tray are in good condition. It is amazing where water under pressure can reach, and check that the drain-hold in your shower tray can cope with the extra water.

Bath/shower combination mixers
If you have a small bathroom you need not miss out on a shower. The bath/shower combination mixer – or blender shower – looks attractive and a good quality screen fitted on the side of the bath should work well.

Choose a good quality mixer with an automatic diverter which cuts

123

off the shower, diverting the water to the bath taps, if the supply pressure drops to an unsafe level.

Cubicle (independent) showers

Where you have the space, a mixer/blender shower in a separate cubicle is a boon for easing morning congestion in the bathroom. Different types are available for vented systems with water storage tanks or 'invented systems', where both cold and hot water are supplied at mains pressure. The heart of this type of shower is the mixing valve, in which water temperature can be either manually (mechanical mixers) or thermostatically controlled.

Thermostatic showers are designed to stabilise any temperature changes that may occur while the shower is operating; these are often caused by changes in water pressure or flow rate when taps are operated or WCs are flushed.

Mechanical mixers are less expensive than thermostatic mixers, but do not offer the same degree of temperature control, and therefore safety. This type of mixer valve ideally needs balanced water pressures to be safe. Check with a plumber that your system is suitable.

Electric showers

The instantaneous electric (or gas) shower is popular because it heats water directly from the mains as it is used. You can have constant hot water, without waiting for it to warm up if you are last in the queue, or if the water heating has been switched off. An electric shower can be economical, both to buy and to run.

Buy an instant shower with an adequate power rating. The shower flow is limited by the ability of the heater to raise the water temperature to comfortable showering levels and in winter mains water can be pretty cold. That is when you need a high rated heating unit.

- Different types of shower use different amounts of water, depending on the pressure under which water is supplied to the shower head, or the ability of the heating system to raise water temperature to the desired level. The more water a shower uses, the higher its running costs. In descending order of water consumption we have power showers, mains pressure (invented) systems, mixed/blender showers and instantaneous showers.

- Not all imported showers on the market are suitable for UK conditions. Make sure that the product you choose is designed to fit UK plumbing, operate on typical UK water pressures and comply with UK water by-laws.

The bidet

Although bidets have a distinctly continental image they have long been accepted in the UK and are included in the product and colour ranges of all the quality British sanitary-ware manufacturers.

There are three basic types of bidet, and these depend on the method of water supply.

Over-rim supply bidets have hot and cold water supplied either through a mixer tap or, less often, through two separate pillar taps mounted on the rim. The mixer tap often has a nozzle which can be swivelled in order to dispense water in various directions.

Under-rim supply bidets have water supplied through a channel in the rim which, it is claimed, warms the area you sit upon. Because it is possible for water in the bidet to rise above the inlet level, its plumbing must comply with the strict back-flow prevention requirements of the water by-laws.

Ascending spray bidets have a nozzle set in the bottom of the bowl which can be operated to provide an upwardly directed cleansing spray. There is a choice of 'dedicated' hot and cold water supplies, separate from the rest of the household plumbing.

For hygiene reasons it is vital that water from a bidet cannot get back into the mains water supply. When fitting either an under-rim supply or ascending spray bidet it is advisable you contact your local water company to determine the exact plumbing requirements before you commit yourself to the project. There are heavy fines for contravention of the water by-laws – and it is the user who is liable. Don't take chances.

HOW TO SAVE MONEY WITHOUT TEARS

TONY LUSH

Tony Lush runs the self-build training and consultancy company Juvan Courses and is also publicity officer of the Association of Self-Builders. He has a degree in physics and taught for ten years before setting up a building company.

How and where you can save money when building your own house is bound up with that all-important question about how much of the work you intend to do yourself. This chapter is aimed at those who intend to do at least some of the work on site themselves, rather than delegate it all to professionals.

The best way to save money on a house that is managed by a third party is to be sure you have chosen exactly the right person to manage the job: someone who understands what you want, and how much you have to spend.

If you are intending to do a certain amount of the work yourself it may be better to decide which work can most profitably be done by you and which is best left to tradespeople.

Some of you will want to tackle all the work and some will tackle certain specific sections of the building, purely because that is what you want to do. I understand that and good luck to you, although I suspect you will find a lot of people who think you are barking mad. If you are in this dedicated group, please read on, even if what I say is going to be overruled by what you intend to do.

There is no way any ideas I put forward can be the definitive money-saving tips; each of you will have your own preferences and strengths, and you would be far better to work with these, rather than try and be a jack of all trades. If you are a superb manager you might be wasting your time driving round collecting materials for the site. However, if you are the type of person who cannot manage your way out of a paper bag, do the running around.

I cannot overemphasise the importance of understanding how the site works and knowing what is happening. I am not suggesting that you know everything about every trade, but a good overall knowledge will help you to appreciate what is going on and how well the job is progressing. There are various ways of gaining the relevant knowledge: you can read books, watch other self-build sites and talk to the tradesmen, talk to other self-builders, or go on training courses.

Organisation is the key to saving money. It is no good saving £40 on a thousand bricks if they arrive a day after they are needed by a bricklaying gang, if they cost you £50 a thousand to transport, or don't match the ones you already have.

This may seem to you an obvious statement but think about it in other contexts. I know people who will drive five miles to save 15 pence on a bag of cement; is it worth the petrol, time and effort? You need to decide. It will depend partly on how many bags you buy and what you could do with the time when you are not driving. These may seem facile comments but I am sure you understand what I am getting at. It is all a matter of time and effort best spent.

If you intend to organise the build yourself, you need to know *what* to organise. Work carefully to the programme (schedule of works – see pages 140–42) that has been drawn up; use it to order materials and book tradesmen as necessary, remembering to give people plenty of notice: you cannot expect the ground worker to leave half way through one job just because you have asked the Building Regulations inspector to inspect the footings a week too early.

Tradesmen can often be late arriving, not an hour or two late but a week or two: it is very hard to time how long each job will take, and if each job overruns by two days it does not take many jobs to put the schedule out by two weeks. When you are ranting and raving at a tradesman for not turning up on time, bear this in mind. If you give them a hard time they will make up their lost time by missing your job out completely.

Materials can be as much of a problem to organise as people. Order bricks in plenty of time and have a place to store them where they will not be in the way and where they can be kept dry. This applies to most materials, so check the delivery time well in advance and then again a week or two before you need the order, just in case. But do not order bulk deliveries of perishable materials like cement, plaster or plasterboard too early. They need to be stored carefully or they will deteriorate rapidly.

The tradesman will not only need the main bulk materials; there will be other requirements. Work to the bill of quantities if one has been provided, but remember to ask the tradesman if he requires any particular item or materials. Most tradesmen have their own preferences, or should I say idiosyncrasies; provided these do not affect the longevity or quality of the final job, that is fine. Try to ensure the tradesman has what he needs, a water butt for the bricklayer, scaffolding for the plasterer, and a power supply for most of them. I have found it best to ask each individual what he needs before he arrives on site. You will be surprised how much the list varies: save them time and you save money.

If you are organising the site, take care to do it well. We have found that an hour or so each evening after the tradesmen have left is usually well spent just sorting things out. *Not* interfering, but stacking bricks on to the scaffold, moving the odd box of nails inside, out of the rain, and covering bags of cement: you will be surprised how much mess a team of builders can leave after a day's work.

Never underestimate how important it is to have the builder on your side, and to use his knowledge. A good relationship with the tradesmen can save a lot of money; a bad relationship is just too horrible to consider.

UNDERTAKING THE WORK YOURSELF

I find it hard to advise how much work you should do yourself. If we are considering the job from a purely financial point of view, it may be better to go to work and let the tradesmen do the job. However, if you have not got a job, only employ the people you really need. You can do these calculations far better than I can. That said, it is a waste of time and money to employ tradesmen to do tedious preparatory work that can be done by you, provided you know how. As an example, wiring a house is a job for a tradesman: he will have to test the installation and verify that it meets the regulations. But there is a lot of basic 'carcassing' that can be done by the likes of you and me. Carcassing is running cables, cutting holes in joists, cutting out recesses for metal back boxes, and fitting them. If you have the right arrangement with a tradesman, he will show you how to do a job and then let you get on with it. Just a word of warning: if you have been quoted for a completed job, the fact that you helped will make the tradesman's job easier but he may not charge you any less.

So far I have been talking about general cases, to encourage you to think over how to plan the build. Perhaps now is the time to consider some specific tasks. Remembering that you know your own ability better than most, bear in mind that you are building a house that will need to pass test and inspection before it can be lived in. Poor or incorrect preparation work for tradesmen may cost more than a job being done completely by tradesmen. I am not trying to dissuade you from the task: I am saying beware if you do not think you can do it!

Site work/Foundations

The ground work is best done by the digger driver, with an engineer to do the setting out. However, if you are confident, have a go. By now you should have spent many hours looking at the plans and deciding how to start the job. If you haven't, now is the time to make sure that you understand the plans before you cut the first sod.

You must adhere to the plans as far as location on the site is concerned: if the house is to start 1m in from, and parallel to, a boundary, that is what it must do – not 1.5m in and running at an angle to the boundary. Use temporary stakes driven into the ground as a rough guide for the location of the house. Often the level of the drains will dictate the level of the house. If this is not the case, you will need to decide on the finished floor level, remembering that it is 150mm above the final ground level. Mark this level well away from the work area.

129

Often the digger will remove all the topsoil, if there is any, and pile it up in one corner, so make sure that this is not in the way of anything else that is going on. Save the topsoil for your garden if possible. You will need plenty of storage space around the site for bricks, gravel, sand, etc, so ask the driver to flatten off a few other areas to help storage and access. Any surplus soil or base material will need to be carted away: this is an expensive task as you will have to pay for cartage and tipping unless you know a local landowner who wants some infill material. So ask around; it could save a fortune if it is not too far away and the lorry driver can get into the site.

Once the site is levelled you can begin to mark out the location of the house. If you do this yourself, take time over it. There is a dual problem here: the digger driver will not want to hang around for a day while you mark out the footings, but he will charge travelling time to and from the site.

Talk over the problem before you start and see what arrangement you can come to. Never rush the preparatory work: get it right. I would use a laser level to get the levels right, and profiles set well away from the work area to set out the walls of the house. There is no reason why with a lot of care you should not be able to mark out the foundations for the digger driver, as long as you know what you are doing. You cannot be too accurate with this job especially if you are building a timber-frame house: often the tolerances for the foundations are plus or minus 5mm.

Check and double check the levels and the setting out with someone who knows what is happening. Decide where the drains will run so that the soil pipe can be set in the foundations. The same applies to water, electricity, gas and telephone cables: it is far better to bring them in underground if you can. If the services are not available at this stage, ask the supplier of the service what sort of ducting is needed.

Once the profile pegs are driven into the ground as far away from the working area as possible, stretch lines between them. At this stage, check again to ensure that the rooms are square and the right size. When you are sure that all is correct, mark the location of the lines on the ground by dropping sand over the line so that it leaves a trail on the ground. Remove the lines and the digger driver can then start digging the foundations using the sand trails as a guide. The building regulations inspector will need to inspect the trenches before the concrete is poured and will need at least 24 hours' notice.

Don't forget to book the ready-mix lorry in plenty of time. When the foundations are dug, go round and drive pegs into the sides or the base of the trench to mark the final level of the concrete foundations: once the concrete starts to flow, there is no more time for niceties. Now, with plenty of help from your friends, you are ready to pour the concrete. Work as accurately as you can.

The next stage will be to brick up the foundations to damp proof course level, and then lay the oversite. Again, a good deal of organisation is required here: the levels are crucial and the method of flooring you have chosen will need to be taken into consideration.

Once you have organised up to this initial stage, you will have a good idea of how well you are coping. I have gone into considerable detail here because it is the make or break stage: if you can pull this together, get it right, and still be smiling, you can consider doing the rest of the work. If, however, you made lots of mistakes and hated every minute of it, perhaps you are not cut out for this job. If all this seems too much for you, it may be money well spent to employ a contractor to get you to this stage. Once you start building upwards above the ground, things get more exciting – burying £2000-worth of concrete in the ground is not my idea of fun!

Walls

Bricklaying seems so much quicker when it is done by a bricklayer, partly because he does it all the time. You may eventually be as quick as a professional but by then you will have completed the house. If you are building a timber-frame house, when and how rapidly you build the brick skin is up to you. You will need scaffolding for the bricklayer, which will need to be increased in height at certain stages so that the brickie can keep working. Very often the gang of bricklayers will work in conjunction with a scaffolding firm who will erect the next 'lift' when it is needed. It does not take long to erect the next lift of scaffold, but any halt in the job is expensive.

When you are negotiating the price with the bricklayers, they may give some discount if you offer to provide certain facilities, like labouring for them or supplying ready-mixed mortar on site each day.

Roof

Once the walls are up, get the roof on and then you can work inside the house as well as outside. If the roof is being built *in situ*, pay for a good carpenter to do the work. But if trusses are being used, then, as long as the scaffolding is good and you have an easy way of getting the trusses on to the roof, and plenty of labour, have a go yourself. The manufacturer of the roof trusses will supply details of where to locate them and how to fix them. This is not difficult, but for some sections of the roof double trusses are required and you need to know where these are and how far apart the trusses need to be. The bracing is important, but simple enough to do once you know where it goes.

Roofing is one of those jobs that get quicker with experience. It is quite easy to do yourself providing you are prepared to climb ladders all day with arms full of battens or tiles. Before you start to felt and batten the roof it is important to get any gable ladders built, and the fascias and

barge boards cut and fitted properly. If you are not sure, get a carpenter to do this and you may then be able to persuade him to show you how to do the felting and battening. Once the battens are in place, it is a matter of hard work putting the tiles or slates on. Modern tile systems with dry eaves are robust and very easy to fit; however, you need to calculate the size to within a few millimetres if the dry eaves are to fit properly. This is worth doing to save time and the inconvenience of building eaves with soffit boards and mortar undercloaking.

One advantage with deskilling the building trade is that the amateur can have a go; spend a little more on materials but save the labour cost. Having said that, lead flashing, should it be necessary, is one of those jobs I leave to a plumber. Many roofs are designed to avoid flashing altogether. Valleys can be lined with lead or with ready-made reinforced fibreglass sections, which again are easy to fit and look as attractive as lead.

Once you have got a roof over your head you are now spoilt for choice: work can be going on outside and inside and you can decide which tasks you intend to tackle yourself and which you will leave to the tradesmen. I assume that if you have a roof over your head you have windows in place. If for one reason or another you have not, it is worth making up frames of 75 x 50mm timber and polythene to go into the window openings and keep the rain out. From now on, the inside of the house must not get wet.

First fix

The first fix of any trade is the work that is done before the finishing starts, but after the main structure has been completed. First fix carpentry is quite a straightforward job that requires knowledge but not a great deal of skill. It includes fitting floor joists, stair trimmers and stud partitioning. There is also first fix electrical and plumbing work to be done.

This is often referred to as 'carcassing'. It is simply a matter of deciding where each appliance is to be situated and then running the correct size pipes and cable to it.

Now is the time to decide on the electrician and plumber you intend to use and ask them to plan the systems for the house. If this has already been done, ask them in to indicate where the cables or pipes should run and what size they should be. Try to imagine the location of each appliance and how the room will look. The family should decide how the rooms are to be arranged, so that the location of a radiator or power point will not disrupt your plans for interior design. Once the cables are run and the plastering finished it is hard to move a light, a switch or a radiator, so plan with care. Radiators are always on the wrong wall, so why not consider under-floor heating?

As the house takes shape, your plans for it may change. If you are going to make alterations, make them as early as possible but remember that they may cost extra money and they may need the approval of building regulations or planning. Altering the location of a radiator at this stage is no problem but suddenly deciding to go for under-floor heating may completely alter the floor structure. The advantage of asking the trades-man in to plan the system is that when he comes to connect up ('second fix') he will be familiar with the system.

When cutting holes in structural timber, such as joists and studs, take care not to weaken them too much. While you are building the house, plan where the cables and pipes are to run. We seem to add them as an afterthought which makes it almost impossible to re-route them should we need to.

Do not run cables and pipes together or in the same ducting. As far as plumbing goes, I am beginning to feel that plastic pipes are a good idea and a saving. Although the fittings are more expensive, there are less of them because the pipes are in far longer runs without a join, and the connections are push fit, which means no spanners and no blow torches. The fact that they are flexible means that the plastic pipe is easy to pull in through holes in the joists.

Even if you are not going to fit one at this stage, run the pipework in for a built-in vacuum cleaner, then if you do want one all you need to do is buy the unit. The pipework fitted at this stage will cost £50–£60, more if you have a large house. Remember and run all the other little luxuries, like coaxial cable for TV aerials, telephone cables and burglar alarms. Some insurance companies will give a discount if a satisfactory burglar alarm system is fitted, so why not contact a few and see what they require while it is still relatively easy to run the wires?

It is a building regulations requirement that every new dwelling has at least one mains-powered smoke alarm fitted. If you are fitting the interlinked type alarms, the cables should also be run in now.

Finishing or cladding

The time to fix the cladding, that is, the walls, floors and ceilings, is when the first fix joinery, electrical and plumbing work has been completed. Ceilings and some walls are clad with plasterboard, while some walls are wet plastered. Plasterboard can either be dry lined or finished with a skim of plaster. Drylining simply involves taping and filling the joints in the plasterboard and then painting or papering over them. This can be done on both walls and ceilings. Plasterboard not only provides a decorative base, but also a great deal of fire resistance. To ensure that this is not impaired, fix the board according to the specifications and ensure that the recommended thickness is used. Fixing plasterboard is easy, especially if you use a cordless screwdriver with the proper chuck. These chucks hold the rust-resistant plasterboard screws so that they are easy to start into the board, then, when the head is the right distance below the surface of the board, they release their grip on the screw. A perfect job each time, once you get used to it.

I can see no reason why you should not do this job but, before you do, get a quotation from two or three specialist drylining firms: you may find that they will dryline your house more cheaply than you can buy the board.

Block walls are given an undercoat of plaster about 13mm thick, and then skimmed to give a satisfactory finish. Plasterboard can be skimmed with a finish plaster to give a smooth finish. Wet plastering is a hard and skilled job; take my advice and get it done by a plasterer.

Floorboards can be of various types: if you are intending to use decorative timber, I would fit these as late in the proceedings as possible, otherwise you may find that they are damaged. Failing this, protect them with hardboard until the work is finished. Chipboard or MDF tongued and grooved flooring is inexpensive and robust. Use only flooring grade material: never try to save money by short-cutting on material quality. For ease of work, it is better to fit these before the walls and ceilings are finished. I can see no reason why this job cannot be done by you, but ensure that the flooring is well fixed down and that you leave access to cables and pipes. Once the boards are down, mark the location of the cables and pipes: this may help to prevent you piercing them with a nail later on in the proceedings.

Second fix

This is where the money either disappears or can be saved. Up to now all the work you have done has been structural and it would be unwise – no, stupid – not to do this work with good quality materials. The second fix is little more than elaborate decorating. And so if, for example, you cannot afford 7 inch skirting, go for standard 100mm (4 inch) bullnose until you can afford the better material.

Second fix joinery is a lovely job if you have the time and skills to do it. It involves fixing stairs, skirting, architrave, doors, window boards; in fact, all the finishing touches. With some of the power tools now available the job gets easier and more accurate. If you are a DIY fanatic, think of the tools this job will entitle you to buy! A wonderful excuse: many a workshop has been stocked using the second fix as an excuse to buy all the tools you don't really need, but have always wanted.

Second fix electrical work involves putting on the electrical socket outlets, fitting the fuse box, etc. Although this is an easy job, it will need to be inspected by the person who is testing your electrical installation, so if you do the connections it may pay to leave the fittings off until they have been looked at.

Again, why buy the best at this stage? If money is a little short buy the materials that will do the job adequately, and change to automatic dimmers, etc later.

Second fix plumbing can be expensive: it includes the central heating boiler, bathroom appliances, radiators, taps, etc. Do not be tempted to skimp on the boiler. You can always change radiators for a more pleasing design later, should you so wish, but not the boiler. I am a great believer in making the plumbing as easy to work on and maintain as possible: fit service valves to isolate each tap – then it is a simple matter to change a tap later on. Run the 'drain off' for the heating system to the outside so that all you have to do is open a tap and drain the system without the house having dripping hoses running through it. It also pays to plan zone controls for the heating at an early stage. It is about now that the care you took planning and laying the drains pays off, you hope. If you have got the 110mm soil pipe in the right location, the job of connecting up the plastic soil and vent pipe is relatively simple. If it is wrong it is hard work, so take the easy way out and call in a plumber.

MATERIALS CHOICE

It is worth considering the quality of materials and where you buy them. In many cases the quality of structural material is specified by the designer of the building, the building regulations and the codes of practice. Do not be tempted to skimp on these just because they will not be seen. Ensure that tradesmen are not using materials that are not specified. If you are not sure, check the specifications supplied with drawings. If these do not exist or are unhelpful and you still have doubts ask the Building Control Officer. Building Control is there to help you and it has been my experience that they are only too willing to do that, certainly where the choice of material affects the structure of the property.

Shop around: basic materials vary dramatically in price. I make out a list of the items I need and fax or post them round to various builders merchants for a quote. Before you accept a price:

- Find out when the money is needed. Before delivery is often the case, but this means that you have no recourse if the items do not arrive on time, are faulty or incomplete.
- Start an account with the firm: this gives you a few weeks to pay.
- Take care to ensure that the price includes VAT.
- Ask how much extra for delivery and how much discount you will get if you collect it yourself.
- With some of the heavier materials such as blocks and bricks it is worth enquiring about off-loading facilities. If you have to employ a gang to off-load it will cost you more money.

The message is try to find the hidden costs that may catch you out. There must be a way of ensuring that the goods arrive on time, but I have never found it. Usually, if you plan properly, they arrive as and when you need them, but if you have a gang ready to put the roof trusses on but the trusses have not yet arrived it is going to cost you money and time. This is a good example because it is not easy to store roof trusses and it is often easier to take them from the lorry to the roof in one day. If you find a foolproof way of ensuring that you get the materials on time let me know, please!

LABOUR CHOICE

Good tradesmen are a blessing; bad ones are a real problem. Unfortunately, we usually only hear the hard luck stories. There are more good stories about tradesmen who have helped far more than was necessary. The best way to find a good tradesman is by recommendation. Ask people you know in the area; call in at houses that are being built and ask. If you cannot get recommendations ask for references and go to look at some jobs the tradesman has done.

It may seem a wonderful idea to knock prices down until you have a real bargain but beware: an unhappy tradesman is not going to do a good job; in fact, he may go and do a job that is paying the right rate and leave you in the lurch. It is hard to decide whether to pay by the job or by the hour. Hourly pay is a little dangerous if you do not know how much work to expect in a day, but if you intend to pay by the job make sure that the tradesman understands exactly what he has to do and that the necessary materials are there. Otherwise, you may find a few extras creeping in. Do not expect the small jobs to be done free; the sort of 'while you are here could you just build a garden wall' attitude is just not on.

Do not pay in full before the job is complete: your cheque book is possibly the best assurance that the work is done well and on time.

KNOW WHAT YOU ARE DOING

I am not suggesting that you become a builder overnight but, if you are intending to manage the job, the more you understand the better. Books are a good source of information and so are other building sites. There are one or two companies running courses aimed at self-builders, and, of course, there are the technical college courses for various trades. Become well informed, but do not start arguing with a craftsman about how the job should be done unless you are sure it is being done wrongly: there are many ways to build properly.

REGULATIONS

You will need to comply with a few sets of regulations, and it makes good financial sense to know what they are before you start. This knowledge may help you to avoid a fine or having to re-do a job.

Planning permission is obvious, but do comply; don't think that once the plans are passed you can do what you like. I have spoken to quite a few people whose plans stipulated a certain building material: roof tiles are a good example. They then found a cheap source of a slightly different tile which they used, only to find the planning man on the doorstep asking them to change the tiles.

Building controls are there to ensure that your house is structurally sound, well ventilated, safe from fire, hygienic and warm – in fact, many of the things you require. If Building Control has specified a certain material, use it – not a substitute that seems to be all right at the time.

One house I know was built using wall ties that did not comply with the required standards, and when the Building Control Officer saw them he insisted that the walls were taken down and re-built using the proper ties. Who pays for that?

Electrical installation regulations are set by the Institution of Electrical Engineers (IEE). Since January 1993 the regulations have gone into their sixteenth edition. For your own safety, be sure the work complies. No electrician would sign off a job that does not comply with the sixteenth edition. These regulations include proper installation, cable sizes and earthing.

The Water Authority by-laws are in force to prevent wastage and contamination of water. They are strictly enforced regulations and heavy fines can be levied if they are not adhered to.

The Control of Pollution (Amendment) Act 1989 and the Controlled Waste (Registration of Carriers and Seizure of Vehicles) Regulations 1991 control the dumping and carriage of waste material. Contravention of these can involve a fine of up to £20,000.

It may seem expensive to insure the property while you are working on it, but there are thieves about who will steal the most amazing things, and accidents do happen; so be well insured.

I am sure that none of you would consider building a new home that was not properly certificated. This can be done by an architect, an NHBC builder, some insurance companies (Foundation 15) or an engineer. You will have a job selling the house and raising finance on it if it is not.

CHAPTER 9

SITE MANAGEMENT FOR SELF-BUILD

PHIL BIXBY

Phil Bixby is an architect who graduated from Oxford Polytechnic in the early 1980s and founded Constructive Individuals, the architectural project management and training organisation.

Site management for self-build is a curious cross between art and science. It is rooted in the simple business of making the most of information available to you, using this information to make decisions, and then communicating those decisions to the appropriate people. Simple? Well, in principle it is.

As all your friends will doubtless tell you, building a home for yourself is a complex business, and a lengthy one. But, as the Chinese philosopher said, 'the longest journey begins with one step'.

THE FIRST STEP: DRAWING UP A PROGRAMME

Way, way before you actually start on site you must draw up a bar chart, or programme, for your project. In addition to being an essential tool for convincing funders that you have thought about your project, it will show you what needs to happen when, and how long it will take.

First, you must organise your thoughts and set targets. What is the scope of the work to be undertaken? Quickly dispose of grey areas such as 'we might do this or we might do that' by dividing the project into phases or options, and then deal with each one. Once you know what the target – or each target – is, set about finding out what work is involved in implementing it.

If you don't know what is involved in a piece of work, ask someone who does! Self-builders often have a fear of appearing ignorant in front of tradesmen, but asking straightforward people straightforward questions is a useful skill. If you ask tradesmen to quote for elements of work, when they come to look at the job (and you should make sure that they do come to look at the job), don't just stand around smiling pleasantly: ask questions, listen to the answers, and make the most of their experience.

Once you have basic information, start to construct a tool for yourself – a bar chart. This starts off as a simple list of activities, or tasks, in any order. The first refinement is to get the jobs into a logical order. Again – think. If you don't know – ask. Is the plasterboarding done before or after the door linings? The electrics before or after the plumbing? The drains before or after the foundations? Find out. Once you have an order, break each job down into all its components.

When you have done this, on a suitably sized sheet of paper, set up a horizontal scale in suitable chunks – days, weeks or months. Then find out how long each task will take, using your finely honed questioning skills as outlined above. Always try to get as close to reality as possible; advice in a book may be useful, advice from a helpful tradesman who has looked at the job may be better, and an estimate of time from the subcontractor who will be doing the job is best of all. When you know, note the duration against each task.

For the next step, work out the relationship between tasks. Generally, each successive task will start either after the preceding one has finished, or a set period after the preceding task has started. Again, pick the brains of those who know. If you want to practise this kind of ordering of tasks on something more familiar, think how you would get the components of a meal prepared, cooked and on the table at the right time. Professional project managers have a whole repertoire of jargon for this kind of stuff but you only need to use the principles of it.

Represent the timing and duration of each task with a bar (hence 'bar chart'). Once you have done this, you will start to notice some interesting things. For example, when you take everything into account the job may take longer than you first imagined. You will start to see those tasks which have a greater 'knock-on' effect if they are delayed – this is the 'critical path'. It is this chain of tasks which follow one from another and set the overall programme for the project.

At this stage, you can expand your bar chart to give information on materials, the requirements for each task, to give you the cost of each, and hence the cash flow projections for the project. This financial management is discussed in more detail below, but it is important to remember that your bar chart can be marked up with dates when materials must be ordered, so that they will turn up when you need them.

Task	Time	Mon	Tue	Wed	Thu	Fri	Mon	Tue	Wed
Site preparation									
Clear site undergrowth	½ day	▓							
Scrape site with JCB	½ day		▓						
Clear muck away	½ day			▓					
Set out for drains	½ day			▓					
Excavate for drains	1 day				▓				
Foundations									
Set out	1 day			▓					
Excavate for trenches	1 day					▓			
Inspection by Building Control Officer							X		
Pour concrete	½ day						▓		
Brickwork up to dpc	2 days								▓
Lay drains below floor slab	1 day								
Ground floor									
Lay and compact hardcore	1 day							▓	
Sand blinding	½ day								
Lay damp-proof membrane	½ day								
Place reinforcing mesh	1 day								
Install expansion board	½ day								
Pour concrete	1 day								

Example of project programme

MONITORING AND UPDATING YOUR PROGRAMME

One of the central skills of site management is the ability to take your programme and make it work on site; too often the programme is quickly seen to be inaccurate once work starts and is then ignored. The correct approach is to use information on progress to update the programme so that it is always current and useful.

How is this done? Find ways of getting accurate information on how long jobs are taking, what materials are being used and what costs are being incurred. A basic minimum is to keep a page-to-a-day site diary going, noting:

- Who is on site each day, and for how long
- What work is done, and who did it
- Any deliveries
- Any visitors (eg Building Control, reps, etc)
- Any accidents or incidents (but also keep an accident book).

In addition to being a good record to refer back to about who was around and when (eg 'Further to your letter regarding delays I note from the site diary that the materials required were delivered prior to your visit and not as you claimed . . .'), the site diary is a good record of how long things are taking. If you start to realise that every task is taking 50 per cent longer than you planned, either you can revise your programme and make any necessary arrangements regarding funding, insurances, etc, or you can enlist 50 per cent more help in order to keep to programme.

It is important to allow yourself adequate time for project management tasks such as this. A small building firm will have a contracts manager who spends a full working week doing this kind of work, and it is foolhardy to expect that you can do it over dinner or in the bath. Make sure that you have time during working hours when you need to make phone calls, and time well away from a phone when you want peace and quiet to organise your thoughts.

DECIDING WHAT WORK TO DO YOURSELF AND WHAT TO SUBCONTRACT

One of the most fundamental questions that you have to answer for yourself is what are you going to do yourself. There are a number of factors to bear in mind, including:

- Your own level of skill, or opportunities to get the required skills
- Your available time
- The requirements of your funders or insurers
- The effect of project time-scale on cost, which will be influenced by how much money you are borrowing
- The cost of subcontracting work. For example, do you have skilled friends who will do work cheaply or for free?

It is vital that you are realistic about the amount of time you have available for your project. Think about the time required for project management, for site organisation, fetching and carrying, general trouble-shooting and – if you have to – earning a living, and see if anything is left for doing physical building work.

Be realistic about your level of skill; all of us have at some stage said of someone else's work, 'What a mess! I could do better than that.' Could you? If necessary, find out. Go on one of the practical courses available and try your hand.

If you do have time available, you should decide on your policy on subcontracting work. Are you going to subcontract the most skilled jobs, or the ones that require most knowledge, or the most specialist tools? Or do you want to subcontract the boring bits and learn how to do all the fun jobs yourself? The first rule is to check what your funders and insurers will accept; some are very specific about work to be undertaken by 'qualified' or 'suitably skilled' operatives and you may not qualify. Chapter 8 offers specific advice about which tasks may be feasible for you to undertake.

As a rule it is easier to gain knowledge than it is to gain skill; jobs that involve a high degree of understanding of procedure may be easier for you to tackle than ones requiring manual dexterity or an 'eye' for the right way of doing them.

For example, many people shy away from getting involved in the electrics because they assume it is dangerous, but once you understand the basic regulations, first fix electrics is a simple exercise that can save you money if you do it yourself and get an electrician to do the test and connection and perhaps the second fix. On the other hand, tackling plastering as a beginner could be a very frustrating business indeed and you may still need thick wallpaper to disguise the results.

Working with subcontractors

It is highly likely that you will have subcontractors – building tradesmen – on your site at some time even if you undertake the bulk of the work yourself. If you are purely project managing the construction the quality of subcontractors will be even more vital. Getting good work from subcontractors comes from:

- Finding good, appropriate subcontractors in the first place, then . . .
- Making clear agreements with them about what they are doing and you are providing, and once they get on site . . .
- Managing them on a day-to-day basis.
- Most of this (indeed, most of the whole business of successful self-build) is about good communication.

Where do you start? Well, the Yellow Pages should be a last resort. Ask friends, colleagues and other self-builders whether they have had work done, and done well. Look out for small local builders and find out who they subcontract trades to. Meet subcontractors as people, and try to judge whether they are sane and sensible. Ask for examples of similar jobs they have done, and ask to go and see them.

Once you start getting good tradesmen, the whole exercise becomes easier, as good tradesmen know other good tradesmen. In particular, follow the sequence of trades and you will see how important the previous trade is; for example, a plasterer will like following a good bricklayer, a joiner will like following a good plasterer, and a decorator will like following a good joiner. The same principle applies throughout: consult your programme and all becomes clear!

Clear agreements with subcontractors are vital. Good, straightforward, written agreements following adequate discussion are far more effective than formal contracts with threatening 'penalty' clauses. Always meet tradesmen on site, as problems or site conditions can be spotted. Make sure that you discuss:

- What the tradesman is going to do.
- When you want him to start.

145

- How long you expect it to take.
- Who is supplying materials.
- Who is supplying tools, and whether power (or water or other requirements) is available.
- What preparation needs to be done in advance (make sure that you can do what is required).
- How much the tradesman is getting paid, and when, and in what form – cash? Cheque? Luncheon Vouchers?
- When you will be available to answer questions.
- What standard or quality you are expecting, and who has the final say on this – you? Or your architect?
- Will you be charged VAT?
- Check that they have tradesman's insurance (in case they cause damage to your property).

In addition you must, simply must, discuss income tax. You must agree on one of three ways of dealing with it. If the tradesman can show you a 714 (a card like a credit card but bearing a photo and the tradesman's name) and give you a 715 (a chit like a receipt) in return for payment, you do not need to deduct tax from payments made.

If the subcontractor is a company and can give you a copy of their Tax Exemption Certificate, you don't need to deduct income tax. Otherwise you must deduct tax and complete an Inland Revenue form SC60, in the expectation that in due course you will receive a demand from the Inland Revenue. Do not be persuaded that this won't happen, and don't be talked into paying 'cash with no questions asked' as you can rest assured that questions *will* be asked.

The final thing to ensure is that whatever commitments you make with regard to payments, you must be totally sure that you can fulfil them. This depends on your doing cash flows and making sure that you have money coming in to cover the cheques going out. Apart from any considerations of integrity and honesty, if you expect tradesmen to come back to sort out odd jobs or problems it is important to make sure that they leave site happy.

This is where many people come unstuck. We hear all about cowboy builders, so don't become a cowboy client.

Once the tradesman starts work on site it is vital to keep a good working relationship going. The following anecdote illustrates the point. One self-builder I know subcontracted the facing brickwork to his timber-framed bungalow. It was winter and the work was done during a week when the self-builder was working at his normal job; he visited in the evenings (by torch light) and all seemed well. Unfortunately, in the cold light of day the following weekend he realised that the bricklayer had been doing a very rough job and the appearance was awful, but by this stage the job was nearly finished and it seemed a bit late to say, 'Take it down'.

It is important to be able to visit the site when work is going on, to answer queries and just to give acknowledgement when a job is being done well. Don't go over the top, don't say something is unreservedly perfect if there may be points that you want cleared up later. Also don't sit on the poor tradesman's shoulder; one self-builder I know was following his bricklayer around with a level and a measuring staff to check his accuracy and was knocking freshly positioned bricks out of position in the process!

To summarise, employing subcontractors is about deciding exactly what you want done, and then ensuring good communication so that both you and the tradesman know what is required.

ORGANISING THE SITE

It is essential to organise the site properly, by planning ahead and by implementing procedures once the work starts. If you don't do this:

- You will run out of space.
- You will store materials incorrectly and suffer wastage.
- You will run a greater risk of accidents.
- You will give the building control officer, your building society, your subcontractors and everyone else the impression that you are amateurish.

So, when should you start thinking about site organisation? Well, my advice would be to take a look at the site plan and think about where everything is going to go before you buy the plot. You may be buying a piece of land which is going to be excessively expensive to build on. Also, think again about access and satisfy yourself that you will be able to

147

get all the materials and plant required to build on to the site. If you are intending to use ready-mix concrete, will you get a lorry on to the site? Are you going to need to move 5000 roof tiles using a wheelbarrow?

It is worth looking a bit closer at the question of materials, deliveries and storage, as the implications of getting it all wrong are expensive. Once you are at the stage of doing a detailed programme, use it to see what materials are going to be turning up and when. For each one, consider the needs in terms of handling and storage.

For example, if you are having plasterboard delivered at some point, you will need to have either plenty of willing bodies around to move it, a very level site and a fork-lift truck, or a JCB with forks on its front bucket. For storage you need to keep it flat and dry, covered, and off the ground. You need to make sure that it doesn't get damaged (particularly if you are using it for drylining, as you won't want to skim over the dents and scrapes) and ideally you want to make sure that you don't have to move it too much, as every time it is shifted it will suffer a little more. It is also very heavy so don't aim to store it all in one big stack on the first floor or it may find its way back to ground level, with half the house on top of it.

You should enquire about delivery arrangements. With heavy materials – for example, bricks and roof tiles – it is possible to ask for mechanical off-load (sometimes called a HIAB), which will at least get it off the back of the lorry. This may cost slightly more or take a little longer to arrange but do consider how long it would take to unload by hand. In general, keeping materials in their pallets or containers helps to protect them. Every time a material is moved you will get more wastage. Try to think of ways of reducing this; for example, have sand or gravel dropped on to a sheet of heavy-duty polythene to stop the bottom six inches of the heap disappearing straight into the ground.

If you don't have any real feel for the scale of the building materials, take a walk around a builders merchants, or visit some friendly neighbourhood self-builders. DIY buffs often think in terms of the scale of bags of filler or boxes of flat-pack units; a pallet of bricks or a works load of concrete is of a different order of magnitude and this will influence the amount of space that must be left on site. A seemingly innocuous pile of sand that has been mis-sited and needs moving may take someone a whole day to move. In addition to being a waste of time, effort, and a proportion of the sand this kind of business is very bad indeed for morale. It will rain on the day it needs moving. The weather knows when you have fouled up.

You will almost certainly have to provide some sort of storage container on site. What form this takes will depend on what you are building and where you are building it. A timber-framed house provides good opportunities for storage of materials as its components are generally assembled immediately upon delivery and the shell is erected quickly. Don't, however, fill the building with materials or you will find it impossible to work in it! Security requirements vary; an isolated rural site may need little security whereas an inner-city site may need barbed wire and a secure lock-up.

As a bare minimum, you will need a dry store, which could be a shed. You will probably need a rack for timber, perhaps made from scaffolding. Make sure that this stores timber level, has a roof, and is suitably sized for the timber you will be using. Don't throw away pallets or scrap timber as these are useful for storing materials off the ground or for packing them to allow circulation of air. In more vulnerable situations you may want a steel secure container which can be hired and which you need to ensure will physically fit on your site. Whatever facilities you require, make sure that you allow for the cost of them in your budget.

Considerations like this lead on to the wider issue of site accommodation. You've looked at accommodating your materials, but what about you and your subcontractors? Where are you going to keep drawings, files or the site phone? A small hut, an old caravan or some similar low-cost space is invaluable. Projects that start in the glorious warmth of a British summer have an unhappy knack of passing through the damp, cold and snow-ridden delights of a British winter, so don't be tempted to set up your site office *al fresco*!

Next, consider where subcontractors are going to have lunch and tea breaks. Unless you have provided some other comfortable space – and strict instructions that it must be used – they will use your house. You will find floors stained by shaken-out mugs, festering tea bags nestling in dark corners, and your new sink will be pre-stained and pre-scratched to save you the trouble of doing it later.

Since we are now dealing with the more sordid aspects of self-build, let's talk about toilets. 'Builders' milk bottle' stories are legion, so I shall simply say that you need to provide some facility for basic human functions or they will take place in the place most convenient for the person concerned. Either hire a site toilet, or get a camping toilet rigged up, make arrangements with neighbours and/or get one of the new house toilets up and running as a priority.

When you are locating accommodation and materials on your site plan, think about site service supplies: water, electricity and telephone. Where do you want these located? Can these locations double up for final service locations? Are these locations safe? Check the requirements of the suppliers.

Assuming that your site is set up so that you have adequate storage and other accommodation, the next step is to make sure that you have procedures to cope with every eventuality. First, you must know in advance where every delivery is going to go on the site. If you are not going to be on site yourself, whoever will take the delivery must know where you want it to be stored. If you don't plan in advance you will end up making snap decisions in the heat of the moment and some of them will be wrong, leading to wasted effort and probably wasted materials and money too.

It is helpful to have fixed storage places for all tools and materials, so that you quickly spot when things are missing.

In addition, you should have a policy of site tidying and 'rubbish' clearance. You should clear debris from the site regularly and have made arrangements for disposing of it by skip or other means. 'Rubbish' is in inverted commas because it often isn't; you should think twice about throwing anything away in case it is of use around the site. Polythene sheet, bits of scrap timber, nails (if still straight) may find a good home on site at least until the project is finished. Materials that really are of no use should be sorted, then you can burn the combustibles and save on skip hire. Don't burn treated timber, as the fumes are toxic, or plastics.

You must be prepared for alarming wastage of some materials. Plasterboard waste, in particular, builds up quickly unless you have someone clearing it away. In the absence of anyone else, make sure that tradesmen are asked in advance to clear up after themselves – expensive, but essential as a last resort.

You should also be prepared for the size of some of the heaps that will rapidly appear. One of the first will be the heap of topsoil from the area of the building, which should be usable on the garden when work is finished. The second will be the spoil from the foundations dig. If you haven't thought how you will deal with these, your site organisation will be doomed from the start.

Summing up: plan your site layout in advance. Think about the handling and storage requirements of every delivery. Work out what is going to happen to wastage and site spoil before it is sitting there staring you in the face, and make sure that site procedures are set up and understood by everyone on the site.

Site safety

An untidy site can lead to accidents. The building industry – and as a self-builder you are part of that industry – is a notoriously dangerous place and the appalling rate of injury and death on building sites has led to tightening up of the regulations in this area.

Any building site falls under the regulations set up and enforced by the Health and Safety Executive (HSE). You must contact them in advance and obtain, complete and submit a form F10 (giving details of the works), as they may well take an interest in you in due course. Free advice beforehand is always better than the heavy hand of the law afterwards. Once you obtain information you should follow the guidance that it contains. You should also be aware of your responsibilities as the person in charge of the building site; if someone is injured or killed you will have to do some very fast talking if you think you shouldn't carry the can.

Setting aside the need to conform to the HSE recommendations, the importance of site safety is a matter of common sense. Lost working time owing to days propped up in bed, or lengthy visits to the local casualty department to repair cut or broken bits of volunteer helpers, all slows down your project and reduces the morale of all involved. Telling the safety officer or Building Control officer that all your family are accident prone and that you've broken your arm 14 times does not impress.

You should consider site safety within the same broad categories as site organisation. First, you should ensure that your site is planned with safety in mind. Do you have room to move materials around safely, and using the most appropriate means? Are temporary power and water lines going to be crushed by site traffic, or dug up by JCBs when the garage foundations are put in? Are you restricting space for storage so that you end up with stacks of tiles three pallets high, all at a precarious angle of dangle?

Next, you should make sure that all accommodation on site is safe. Your timber rack should be properly constructed and not overloaded. Use your eyes and your common sense. When you notice scaffolding poles starting to bend under the load, think of the weight it takes to bend heavy steel tube and imagine what it would do to you if it all finally gave way when you were crawling around in the rack getting timber out. Not a pleasant thought? You wouldn't be the first to die like that.

Make sure that the scaffolding around your building is properly constructed. It should be erected by certificated scaffolders, who should know what they are doing. However, the Construction Industry Training Board (CITB) publishes a good little *Guide to Practical Scaffolding* which you can leave on the site office desk just to let them know that you know. In my experience, it is depressingly rare for scaffolders to turn up, erect and complete a scaffolding correctly without at least a few reminders.

Your site procedures should always have safety in mind. Site mains power must be 110V via a transformer. Don't be tempted to use your 240V DIY tools on site. Never use power tools in the rain. It is sensible always to work on site as pairs; few building tasks are really 'one person jobs' and two people can always look out for each other's safety. Never work totally alone on site. If you did fall off the scaffolding you could lie with your back broken for a long time before help arrived. A helper is always useful when it comes to unplugging a power tool that gets caught in your clothing and jams on.

It is important that, as the person responsible, you set a good example and also try to establish a sensible attitude on site. If you can only easily carry two lengths of stud timber on your own, never try to carry more, even if the subcontract carpenter can comfortably carry four. If it takes you and a friend to carry a sheet of plasterboard, always wait for the friend to help you. Building sites are very silly places to show off how macho you are.

Your site tidying procedures should set out to ensure safety. You should, for example, remove nails from scrap timber to stop them ending up in the palms of your hands or through the soles of your shoes. You should make sure that sheet materials aren't left on scaffolding – a sheet of ply can take off in a strong wind and wreak havoc on its travels. Generally, keep the site clear; rubbish hides holes in the ground and other hazards and encourages a sloppy attitude.

In addition to all the above, there are a few basic dos and don'ts:

- Always wear sensible clothing. General clothing should be warm enough and shouldn't trail around and catch on things. Always use appropriate protective equipment with specialist tools; for example, gloves, goggles and ear defenders with angle grinders. You must, by law, wear a hard hat and steel-toed boots on site. All these warnings apply even if you are project managing a job as you first have a responsibility to instruct people on site to take appropriate precautions, and second, it can take only one site visit to get a rusty nail through the sole of your best office shoes. Don't expect sympathy from the nurse.

- Keep a first aid kit on site. The HSE regulations state what this should contain, but it may be worth supplementing it with extras such as Steristrips and eye-baths. Nurses are quite good at telling you (usually in gory detail and with helpful diagrams) how people commonly harm themselves.

- Keep an accident book. Every accident on site must be recorded there, together with details of how it happened.

- Do ensure that you are adequately insured. You must have Contractors All Risk insurance (CAR) which covers damage to the building, theft of tools, etc. You must also have third party (public) liability cover and employers' liability, and you should display evidence of the latter on site. If someone wanders on to your site and injures themselves, you may be held responsible. It is highly sensible, if you are doing any practical work – even just clearing up – yourself, to take out personal accident insurance. If you are unable to go to work for three weeks because your leg is in traction, it will probably cost you money and may also affect your project. There are combined policies designed especially for self-builders; your building society should be able to advise you.

CONCLUSION

A self-builder friend of mine, who worked as a computer consultant, once described to me how he found it impossible to use computer project management programmes to run a self-build project. He felt there was an 'Ingredient X' in self-build which made it defy normal logic. Self-build certainly requires a particular approach to organisation; because almost every self-build project is different (the house, the site, the background of the self-builder's work and home circumstances, etc), there is no single way to run the project.

There will always be problems. There is absolutely no way to guarantee that a subcontractor will turn up on the day, and do what you asked for. Whoever organises the weather doesn't take bookings. Builders merchants do like their little jokes once in a while. And you, yes you, will at some time forget something you shouldn't have, order something wrong, explain something badly, or lose something you need that will take days to be delivered again.

As a project manager and site manager, you need to rise above mere detail such as this by creating a framework of organisation which copes with problems, delays, bad weather and mistakes. That framework will depend on you and must suit your way of working. It must, however, work in practice, and must allow you to free your head for solving immediate problems by putting lists, plans, procedures and other long-term matters down on paper – in whatever way suits you.

You must plan ahead, and decide what you are going to do, and who you will ask to do the remainder. You must organise your site in advance, know what will be delivered when, and where you want it to go. You must share this information with everyone who needs to know. You must understand that subcontractors are people, and that they like an organised site. You must always consider safety, and never take chances with your life or the lives of anyone who enters your site.

Designing your own home and finding a site are exciting and creative experiences. Building your home – either by doing the work yourself or by directly organising others – is equally a challenging and enlightening process, which can teach you much about a range of issues from construction to your own character. Never stop learning. Never give up on a problem and never duck a decision when it needs to be made. Above all, never let your basic organisation fall apart, and you will see your project successfully through.

CHAPTER 10

ECOLOGICALLY FRIENDLY HOUSING AND ENERGY EFFICIENCY

SIMON CLARK

Simon Clark works as a designer and lecturer for Constructive Individuals; he is an expert on ecologically friendly housing and on specifying and fitting energy-saving features and green products in self-build projects.

One of the pressing questions for the next century will be our relationship with the natural world. What elements should be left alone and which can we afford to develop?

This chapter looks at how we design and build our individual homes with this relationship in mind. Most of the ideas explored are popular and understandable; a few have yet to catch on. By design or accident, nearly all houses will incorporate some of these ideas, yet the starting point for the design of real energy-efficient houses and so-called eco-houses is an integrated plan or strategy.

A strategy for green housing can be looked at under the following headings: siting; natural resource usage; construction systems and materials; energy systems and technology; and building biology.

SITING

Finding the right site for a house is a little like looking for a marriage partner. Time and thought need to be spent, as the house is going to spend the rest of its life there. Once built, the new house and its surroundings will then embark on a potentially eternal marriage that will terminate either because the earth and its creatures reject the house (earthquake, subsidence, dry rot, etc), or because humanity fails to appreciate its design and replaces it with another.

The site you choose must be suitable for building on. All building development manipulates the land and causes damage. We have the choice to limit this damage.

If the site has been decimated by history, it may be possible to restore it to a place of beauty. The green house-developer should undertake a thorough site survey, considering some or all of the following points:

- What is the history of the site? Consider following past traditions if so desired, and gain knowledge of what is to be found in the ground.
- Question the suitability of soil and air for herbaceous, annual and biennial plants and shrubs, particularly to encourage wildlife.
- Conserve the immediate and local wildlife and habitats.
- Potential to use/reuse materials found within the site boundary (trees, clay, shrubs, grasses, the recycling of any existing building materials, etc).
- Potential for plant and food growth on the site.
- Sensory – smells, views and sounds. The siting of building and locating of windows should be planned to make the most of the available views. If required, acoustic levels can be recorded and the house construction designed to screen out unwanted noise.
- Air quality – local and distant industrial emissions. Poor air quality can be determined by the degradation of plants, the existence of deposits

on, for example, building surfaces, the incidence of disease among people in the area and by gaining knowledge of the industrial history of the neighbourhood.

- Soil type and any pollution. On-site soil surveys are the best way to discover soil quality.
- Proximity to harmful, man-made electrical currents. There is now a general acceptance that high voltage overhead electricity cables are detrimental to health. Avoid sites under or near them. Research and tests should be carried out regarding nearby sub-stations.
- Proximity to harmful underground geomagnetic stresses and natural radiation (radon). The National Radiological Board can advise on the location and dangers of radon. Site dowsing or electronic surveillance may be considered in the case of geomagnetic stresses resulting from underground streams and geological faults.
- Renewable energy use/generation potential: flowing water supply for heat pump and/or water turbine installation; wind generated electricity or wind pumps; solar energy capture, either for use 'passively' (see pages 163–4), whereby the orientation of the site and building should be southwards with carefully positioned glazing to allow sunlight into the building, or using 'active' systems, such as solar panels which collect solar radiation and allow water to be heated, or photovoltaic cells which convert sunlight into electricity (see page 170).
- Local natural fuel sources – wood, methane, coal. Should these form the basis of your energy, or heating system?
- Local water sources – surface springs or underground natural reservoirs where wells can be sunk, and rainwater collected.
- Potential for on-site sewage disposal, such as using a septic tank or composting toilet. Reed beds, nature's way of cleansing water, can also be installed. Soil suitability will determine the types of disposal possible on the site.
- Potential for grey waste water irrigation systems, whereby bath water, etc can be directly channelled into the garden.
- Local traditions often determine the design of the house and materials that can be used. The availability of skilled traditional craftspeople may influence what can be built.
- Access to local recycling facilities.

Building Energy a High Energy Rating into a Home by Using Oil Central Heating

The Shell Home Heating Unit explains how to achieve a high Energy Rating on a new home.

Individual house builders have a rare personal opportunity to help both themselves and the environment at the moment of specifying a heating source for their home.

Over a quarter of the carbon dioxide produced in the UK comes from energy used in homes. Insofar as this gas may be linked with the threat of future climatic warming, it makes sense to plan for energy efficiency by consuming the least amount of fuel possible. This also saves money, and may release more funds for increasing insulation and comfort levels at the start of the project.

Vital decisions taken when specifying the construction of the house – aspect, solar gain, insulation, materials, fuel and controls – can all radically affect later running costs. Provided enough information is given, an energy audit should be made on the house at detailed plan stage and corrective action taken to maximise the rating. This in turn will help costs, comfort, and resale value.

Oil scores highest, fuel for fuel, in these energy ratings by virtue of its inherent burner efficiency and low running costs. Any one house heated by oil will always score higher than its twin on a different fuel.

It is an effective way to store energy – a litre of oil contains 10 kilowatts of energy. This high power-to-weight ratio (energy density) makes it available anywhere in the UK, which is why it is a favourite with individual home builders wanting no restrictions on their choice of site.

Performance Standards for Equipment

At the heart of the most efficient system lies a good boiler.

Put simply, all of the boilers sold by firms who are members of OFTEC (The Oil Firing Technical Association) are well-proven high-performance models. They have been used in the half-million plus homes heated by oil and are made by recognised, reputable manufacturers to an efficiency which can reach over 80% in service. According to the particular needs of the new project or boiler replacement, the traditional, "combination" or "package" boiler can be selected – the last two mean that pipework can be simplified. An exciting new addition to this range is the oil condensing boiler, which extracts even more efficiency from flue gas and lends itself well to specialist applications such as underfloor heating. Many boilers no longer need long vertical chimneys, but can operate with a short horizontal balanced flue – which incidentally helps greatly with siting a boiler under a kitchen work top. Boilers can be floor-standing, wall-hung, situated inside or out and even hung on the outside of walls, which is perfect for modernising small cottages. But the best boilers deserve a good start in life. It is vital that a qualified, professional oil distributor installer is involved in the project to attend to details such as the correct pipework connection, combustion air supply and flue installation. All the effort in choosing an ideal system can be wasted by poor water circulation or inefficient combustion, and this is true for all fuels.

The technology behind control systems presents a wider choice than ever before. It is essential, however, to get the basic installation right before embarking on great sophistication. The best results are obtained when circulation is fully pumped for both space and water heating and the controls are arranged to prevent the boiler cutting in and out for brief periods (short cycling). Careful consideration should be given as to how the home is to be used and whether zone controls for different parts of the house, especially conservatories, are appropriate. Such obvious things as an easy-to-use programmer can save hours of frustration for householders later. As in the case of videos, manufacturers seem occasionally unable to make operations friendly to the user! Choose yours with care.

Practical Energy

And how does oil compare to other fuels in its actual use? Most of the questions on this subject range around cost, storage and delivery.

Shell have relied on an independent survey by Sutherland Associates for over five years to track the price of oil against other fuels; oil has averaged out considerably cheaper than its nearest competitor, mains gas. The differential has been about 20% to the favour of oil and appears to be holding steady. Oil is much (about 50%) cheaper than stored gas (LPG). As a result, many new oil boilers are being installed and sales are at a high level.

Shell has long recognised that one of the main cases of unfamiliarity amongst those people considering oil is ordering and delivery. Some very recent Shell research shows that oil users' satisfaction rises with their familiarity with oil and length of usage of that fuel. Here are some helpful indications which show why customers, who know oil, like it:

- *Lowest running costs*
- *Fuel conforms to the British Standard, and is carefully delivered by a local Distributor*
- *Full customer service packs are available and offer personal service including professional boiler installation, commissioning and maintenance. (Shell offer a £25 five year warranty with some new boilers)*
- *A 24 hour emergency breakdown service is available*
- *Storage can now be in maintenance-free plastic tanks*
- *The tank can be up to 30 metres away from the delivery road or driveway*
- *Tanks can be level with or even below the boiler level*
- *Siting is not a problem and can be very discreet, hidden from view*
- *Delivery can be automatic on a "diary" basis, adjusted for the weather*
- *Convenient payment for the fuel can be made by monthly sum, so that cold weather does not bring unusually high invoices*
- *Maintenance is often carried out by the oil Distributor*

For the location of your nearest Shell Distributor who can advise you on OFTEC equipment, local installation/commissioning services and help you with your planning, ring

Freephone 0800-010-100

- Availability of second-hand building materials, eg from specialist merchants or demolition sites.
- Local transport amenities – car, bicycle, train, etc.
- Access to all other essential facilities.

MANIPULATING THE NATURAL ELEMENTS

Good 'green housing' design makes careful use of the natural on-site elements.

Light

A good deal of thought should be given to where you want to position windows, whether in the ceilings or walls, and how much daylight and sunlight is required and where. Modern windows can be as large or as small as you like, at whatever level, to suit your requirements whether you are standing, sitting or lying down.

If possible, all rooms with exterior walls within the house should have windows on at least two walls, and if desired combined with glazing in flat and pitched ceilings, to bring in contrasting tones of light throughout the day. Glazing can also be placed within internal partitions and above doors to 'move' light around the house. Perhaps the greatest house designs are those where the manipulation of light is most sensitive.

Air

Unlike light and solar heat, good quality fresh air and fresh water are limited and subject to pollution. Fresh air inside and outside the house is essential to our well-being. From the point of view of hygiene, human beings need between 30 to 60 cubic metres of fresh air per hour, yet frequently our housing severely restricts this requirement. Older houses tend to ventilate themselves through gaps in the construction, and between the window sashes and the door frames. These days, weather-stripping and sealed double-glazed windows, installed to cut out draughts and save energy for heating, seal this vital access and deny the house its fresh air. This lack of air change leads to the build-up of indoor toxins, causing weariness and respiratory problems, and a greater tendency to become ill, as well as increasing the potential for condensation within the building.

The Swedish model of sealed timber-framed houses and mechanical ventilation is born from the desire to maximise energy conservation and control ventilation rates. In the UK, lower insulation levels, poorer standards of construction and lower consumer expectations mean that energy conservation and ventilation strategies are ill thought out and left to chance.

The green home-builder should first be satisfied with the quality of air in the locality, and then work out, with his designer, a satisfactory passive or mechanical system to safeguard health and liveliness.

Water

There are two principal concerns about the supply of water:

- The limited supply in the face of increasing demand
- The quality of what is supplied.

Demand for public water supply in England and Wales has risen by over 70 per cent over the last 30 years, from about 10,000 million litres per day in 1960 to 17,000 million litres per day in 1990. The scope for further abstraction underground (aquifers) and above ground (rivers) is becoming limited. In recent years, lower than average rainfall has compounded the problem.

Increased housing development also results in increasing water supply infrastructure and drainage facilities, as well as a growing demand on sewage treatment works.

The alternative to developing new supplies is to reduce demand, and/ or recycle, communally within a locality or individually on site, what is used.

The eventual introduction of water meters and a pay-as-you-use policy will finally bring to public attention how we use our domestic water. All domestic water currently used has been treated to drinking water standards, yet, as a household average, less than a third is used for cooking and drinking, which is arguably the only water required to be of this standard. Thus, a variety of supplies could be used to meet the differing demands; for example, mains water for drinking and cooking and on-site recycled water for the remainder.

To use water efficiently, we can begin by reducing the amount flushed down the toilet. In existing flush-type cisterns, anything up to 16 litres (3.5 gallons) per flush can be used. Modern dual-flush cisterns have a 7.5–9.5 litre capacity, whereas some Scandinavian cisterns range between 3.5 and 6 litres. Under current by-laws the maximum cistern capacity should be 7.5 litres. Check your cistern.

Alternatively, modern composting systems based on principles over 30 centuries old and again developed in Sweden, such as the Clivus Multrum and the Lectrolav, involve no water usage, drainage system or chemical usage at all. These reduce by up to 90 per cent the volume of human waste and create organic fertiliser for the garden, as well as involving considerable savings in water infrastructure costs. Ability to manage such a system is the key consideration.

Fine spray shower use can replace bath use, which can use around three times the volume of water; spray head taps, and low water use washing machines are other ways of using water more efficiently. Once water has been used, grey (bath, basin, etc) and brown (WC) water can be treated on site and reused, and a recycling system can be set up.

Grey water can either be channelled through pipework directly into the garden, or cleansed and returned to the home for washing, or flushing toilets. With high quality filters grey water can be drunk, if you can stomach the thought.

The earth's natural recycling system involves used water returning to the sea, evaporating, rising and falling as rain for us to reuse. These days, most water does not go through this cleansing system, and is thus invariably of a lesser standard. A way forward may be the use of reed beds, or Aquatic Plant Treatment Systems (APTSs), which can treat all water on site, and in some cases cleanse brown water to drinking standards, though this is not recommended.

On-site sewage disposal systems need to be considered before deciding on the final siting of the building in order to make maximum use of site gradients and thus the elevation of electric pumps, while the additional plumbing for recycling really ought to be built in during construction.

The quality of mains water varies enormously from place to place, and you ought to test the water using National Rivers Authority procedures. If natural spring sources or underground well water cannot be tapped, indoor filters should be considered and incorporated.

Waterfalls, streams, lakes and ponds all enhance the environment of the green house. Nature brings water to our doorstep via rainfall, and then we go to great effort and expense to build underground sewers to take it away again. Rainwater can be collected and re-used. Its acidic content should be checked to see how drinkable it is. It can be collected at the bottom of downpipes and channelled directly for use in the garden, or collected and piped into the toilet cisterns, or channelled into a mains water system.

The capital costs of some water recycling systems may be greater than conventional systems, yet infrastructure charges to the water authority and annual bills can be reduced.

Heat

Allowing sunlight (solar heat) directly into the house is the simplest and most economic form of natural and constantly renewable heat available.

Passive solar capture

'Passive' solar design, the non-mechanical collection of solar heat, works by considering the building itself as a giant solar panel, focusing heat directly to where it is required. The house should be orientated south as far as possible, and with intelligent design, up to 50 per cent of the south wall can be glazed, optimising collection of solar energy so that solar 'gain' exceeds heat 'lost' through the glazing. The glazing must not be overshadowed by other buildings and trees during the winter months when the sun is low and the heat most needed. This heat energy can be stored in dense floor and walls (often called 'thermal mass') during the winter and, through simple control procedures, is released into the house during the cold nights.

Lightweight structures such as timber frame do not have significant thermal mass, and thus are likely to cool more rapidly during overcast skies than masonry buildings. Good passive solar design will have a substantial amount of thermal mass in the building to maintain a comfortable air temperature for a number of days, with minimal solar input.

Passive solar houses want high levels of thermal insulation to minimise the loss of heat through the floors, walls and roof, thus maximising the contribution made by the sun. It should be remembered that the only reason we need heating systems of any type in the house is because so much is lost and therefore needs to be replaced. As the house is designed to collect sunshine primarily in the winter, it is likely to overheat in the summer. Extended eaves, found more frequently on the Continent, and large windows should be incorporated to allow for high levels of summer natural cooling. Passive solar houses, with their large areas of glazing, tend also to be well lit and thus minimise artificial light energy use.

Active solar capture
The 'active' collection of solar heat, through solar panels and seasonal heat stores, is discussed in the energy efficiency section of this chapter (see pages 169–70).

CONSTRUCTION SYSTEMS AND MATERIALS

Broadly, green house-building materials should be non-toxic, recyclable products which sometimes are the conventional items used by all builders as a matter of course, and sometimes alternatives to the standard manufactured products. The point is that some thought has gone into the choices, which are by no means straightforward, because all that appears green in not necessarily emerald through and through. There are various criteria that we can use to assess building materials, and in the process define the ecological and sometimes the biological credibility of constructional systems. The following points should be considered:

- Purpose and appearance. If something looks out of place or is obviously doing a job it was not intended for, all is not well.
- Diversity of the source and long-term availability of raw materials. For example, timber is a potentially renewable building resource, and to this extent some of the tropical rain forest timber brought into this country from, say, New Guinea will be felled for a short period and then stopped while stocks replenish. Thus, a renewable resource is maintained. But much rain forest timber has historically had, and still currently has, no sustainable management policy and thus ceases, through inadequate management, to be a renewable resource.
- Economic and environmental costs of the extraction of raw materials. For example, clay is quarried to make bricks. The quarry can destroy local habitats and water tables, or scar the landscape. Financially, extraction is relatively cheap; recovery can be expensive.

- Manufacturing processes and toxicity of waste products incurred. For example, the new water-based paints may be less toxic than their solvent-based predecessors, yet the volume and ferocity of the waste product has increased. One tin of polyurethane requires seven tins of waste equivalent during manufacture.
- Locality of material, costs of transporting to site. As a matter of principle, the green house should try to include as many locally made materials as possible.
- The 'cradle to grave' energy costs including manufacture, transport, construction and disposal/recycling.
- Durability of product when fixed. For example, clay bricks are an expensive material to manufacture, with considerable environmental impact, yet the finished product can be very durable, and with care can be recycled, thus having a life spanning centuries. Materials of short life span, yet with less environmental impact in manufacture, may actually be more damaging over time.
- Recyclability of material upon demolition of building. Housing should be detailed to allow for extensive re-use of materials if demolition occurs.
- Propensity to emanate harmful radiation.
- Toxicity of final product to operative and occupant. Many materials, particularly preservatives, glues and paints, give off volatile organic compounds (VOCs) which can be damaging to health, frequently cumulative over time. The architect is responsible for this and should be asked to specify alternatives.
- Local traditions and labour in the area of the plot. Good local sub-contractors will know the building traditions of their area, which may be a good enough reason to design a house that you know your builders can build.

There are many different ways to build and probably more materials than ever before, both natural and synthetic, to choose from. No material will fulfil all the listed specification criteria, yet efforts should be made to ask these questions when deciding which materials to use.

ENERGY SYSTEMS AND TECHNOLOGY

The lifestyle of people in the UK partly reflects the low financial cost of primary energy, for as a nation we use roughly three times as much fuel per person as the world average. Some 30 per cent of the final energy use comes from the domestic housing sector, which is widely regarded as the most energy-inefficient housing stock in Western Europe.

Environment conscious fuels should have a low pollution potential and be able to be burnt/converted efficiently into the form in which we require them, eg space heat or electricity. Carbon dioxide is the usual pollutant bench mark on which fuels are judged, as its release into the atmosphere is linked to the greenhouse effect and resultant global warming potential.

Nearly all UK energy used is obtained from fossil fuels, which are unsustainable as energy sources because they will eventually deplete. Burning them also releases locked-up carbon into the atmosphere as carbon dioxide. Thus, the drive towards ecological sustainability is two-fold: the reduction of fossil fuel use, and the development of renewable energy systems. The pursuit of an energy-efficient house makes sense both ecologically and financially, as future running costs can be substantially reduced with a relatively small increase in capital cost. Furthermore, the uncertainty of future energy costs makes this all the more sensible.

Electricity is clearly the most polluting of mainstream domestic energy used. Present generation methods are based on fossil fuel which is only around 30 per cent efficient. This means that using electricity for heating will produce roughly three times as much carbon dioxide as using a fossil fuel directly.

Electricity does not need to give rise to this much pollution; for example, wind generation creates no carbon dioxide. Wood also has a pollution index of zero. This is true when trees are allowed to grow up again, for while wood releases carbon dioxide during burning, new trees growing in the space of old will absorb roughly the same amount.

Reducing energy use in a house

1. Specify materials and construction processes that require minimum energy input in manufacture and transport.

Research in Switzerland and Germany has indicated that, for most building work completed today, the operating energy consumed over its lifetime still exceeds the construction energy by a fair margin. Of the construction costs, the overall production energy costs of building materials are the most significant, and depend on the cost of extraction of the raw material, manufacturing costs and various transport costs. In energy terms, the recycling of used materials is the most ecologically responsible way to build, as all production costs have been borne and paid for in a bygone age.

Intuitively, we should expect timber to require the least energy to bring it to a form we can readily build with. Yet again, European experience suggests that some masonry systems are at least comparable with timber-frame ones. Buildings using steel, aluminium and fired clay products (tiles and bricks) are particularly energy intensive. Both main-stream construction systems in the UK are relatively energy intensive: cavity walls of clay brick, steel wall ties, a thin slab of plastic foam insulation, aerated concrete inner leaf lined with plasterboard; or plaster-board lined timber-frame, mineral wool insulation, steel ties and clay brick.

An example of low-energy construction is an inner leaf of dense concrete, nylon wall ties, mineral wool insulation and an outer leaf of stone, calcium silicate brick or rendered dense concrete block. Timber-frames insulated with cellulose and clad in timber boarding or render are another low-energy method. The importation of the majority of UK building timber from North America and Northern Europe adds considerably to timber-frame costs, while concrete blocks can be manufactured relatively locally. The use of home-grown timber can be the single most important ecologically minded decision the self-builder can take.

2.   Use good design and construction skills to ensure a durable building. Although energy-efficient design and building techniques are widespread among architects and builders in North America and Sweden (using timber-frame) and increasingly in middle Europe (using concrete block), many of the principles are not understood in the UK. If energy-efficient housing is to be both what it says and durable in the face of a design profession and building industry with relatively little regulation, training or incentive to move forward, individual home-builders need to be exceptionally vigilant both in their choice of designer and builder, and while construction is taking place.

3.   Minimise overall energy use, and in particular fossil fuel use, in the running of the building by maximising the use of renewable energy resources, such as solar and wood. If fossil fuels are used, use the least polluting and most efficient systems, and always use the most energy-efficient appliances and lighting systems.

The energy demands of an average UK house show space heating as the largest component, followed by water heating, cooking, appliance use and lighting. Reduction in space heating costs is achieved by reducing the need for heat. High standards of heat conservation are achieved not only by the general installation of insulation, but by careful design to avoid any uninsulated portions throughout the building (called 'cold bridges'). This last point is frequently ignored by British designers.

Conserving energy – insulation

The type and amount of insulation varies and choices can be made by the self-builder. Software is now available that will estimate running costs based on the thermal design of the property, so designers can advise you in advance of savings that can be made with thicker insulation. The software will also offer estimations of the payback time when considered against capital cost. The additional cost of insulation is partially regained by the reduction in cost of a smaller heating system, allowing financial savings to be made, as well as giving increased comfort.

Insulation strategies are numerous. A construction system should not be chosen until all the various pieces of the design jigsaw have been put together and assessed as a whole.

Further ways to reduce heat loss are the installation of energy-efficient windows and doors. Double glazing should now be the norm in the UK, yet the more insulation is placed in the walls, the more is lost through the windows and doors.

Double glazing with a low emissivity coating, often called 'low E', allowing heat in from the outside yet restricting its passage out again, is readily available in this country and can be fitted in standard window frames at around 50 per cent additional cost of conventional double glazing units. The 'low E' glazing has an equivalent thermal performance to triple-glazed windows, but at a cheaper installation price, and will probably be the next step made by the glazing industry to increase the insulation standards in our buildings. The benefits of triple glazing are principally increased acoustic performance. With good quality windows, doors become the thermal weak point in the external fabric of our house.

I know of no UK companies which manufacture thermally insulated doors, but there are Scandinavian companies which offer windows and doors of exceptional quality, from thermal, acoustic and security points of view, at only a small cost above the better quality UK windows and doors.

Energy conserving design also seals all the gaps *in* the construction to avoid heat loss *through* the construction. Vapour barriers in timber-frame buildings and plaster in block buildings do just this. Yet the more we seal our buildings, even to the extent of pressure testing them (as in Sweden) for leaks, we lose the traditional way our houses were ventilated, and a ventilation mechanism has to be incorporated into the building early on.

If mechanical ventilation systems are fitted, rejected warm air can be passed through a heat exchanger, which removes the heat and adds it to incoming cold air. It should always be remembered that mechanical solutions cost money to manufacture and install, energy to run, and will break down. Thoughtful passive systems can be incorporated and their use is to be encouraged.

Other heat recovery systems include waste warm water, particularly larger quantities from the bath and washing machine, which can be passed through an exchanger, and this heat added to the hot water cylinder. Remember to insulate the pipework.

'Active' solar systems commonly involve solar collectors found on roofs, which capture the intermittent solar heat and, using a transfer medium such as water or oil, transfer this heat via a pump to a storage cylinder. Thus, a secondary solar cylinder within the house can usually provide enough hot water for the summer months, and a valuable 'pre-heat' for domestic tap water in the winter months. The most commonly found solar panel is the 'flat plate' collector, which can be purchased commercially or self-built using DIY guides available from the Centre for Alternative Technology in Macynlleth, Wales.

About four square metres of good quality panel on a roof should provide the average family with around 50 per cent of their hot water needs throughout the year (100 per cent on sunny days, 10 per cent on gloomy days), for a capital cost of between £1200 and £2000. The long payback time of 10 to 25 years means that new systems for retrofitting are not viable, yet as technical developments reduce the price the incorporation of solar systems into new housing becomes economically attractive.

Self-built systems, though probably less efficient than factory-built models, will pay back a lot quicker as capital cost can be as little as £400. An alternative system, more expensive and also the most efficient, is the advanced vacuum tube collector, which responds rapidly to changes in radiation levels and works efficiently with overcast skies. These are not readily self-buildable, so financial calculations should be done to work out the projected payback time if financial viability is your primary objective.

Sunlight, rather than heat, can be used to generate electricity, by the use of 'photovoltaics' (PV cells). PV cells operate without moving parts, noise or pollution, and rely on sunlight's interaction with materials like silicon. PVs are starting to be used in experimental domestic housing in Switzerland, but their use in the UK has a long way to go.

Heating systems

For some radical enthusiasts the objective of the super-insulated, energy-efficient house is to maximise renewable heat gains and minimise the heat 'lost' through the fabric of the building. If these can be seasonally balanced, no heating system will be needed. To achieve this goal, some degree of seasonal heat storage will be required, as in the UK the sun is least abundant at the time of year when we most want to heat our homes.

In the vast majority of cases, some form of heating system will be required. When choosing a system the considerations are:

- what fuel to use;
- what medium is used to transfer heat around the building, eg water, air, electricity cable;
- what sort of heat is required – radiant or convection;
- what sort of heat emitter is used, eg radiator, Rayburn;
- what form of heat emitter control is used.

Fuel

Wood burned in a wood-burning stove is held by many to be ecologically sensible if a local, abundant source of wood waste is available. Wood fires also give off a pleasant rural smell. Alternatively, wood waste incinerators are now available on a domestic scale, where

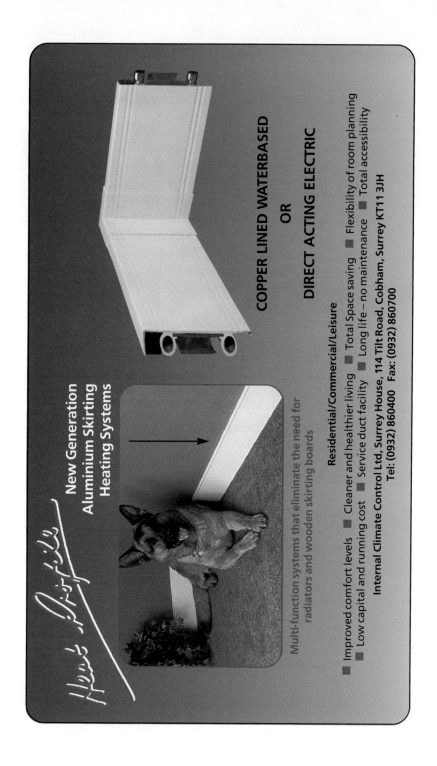

171

water pipework can be connected up to the incinerators. In both cases, efforts should be made to capture the heat given off in the flue gases and recirculate this around the house.

Natural gas is the most efficient fossil fuel in terms of its conversion to usable heat. Either combination boilers which only heat water as it is used, or condensing boilers are considered the most energy efficient. The condensing boiler, running at an efficiency level of up to 90 per cent, uses up to a third less fuel than similar-sized conventional boilers, thus reducing running costs as well as carbon dioxide emissions. They are more expensive, yet the payback time can be less than four years, so retrofit as well as new-build projects are suitable for their installation. The Government are currently running a £200 rebate scheme if you fit a condensing boiler. (Contact British Gas for information.)

Condensing boilers can also run off oil, which is usually the most cost fluctuating fuel, yet they offer the most economical solution if oil is to be used.

Owing to the polluting and inefficient way in which the majority of UK electricity is produced, this fuel should be avoided for space heating unless the source is directly from renewable (eg local wind farm or hydro) sources, and not via the grid.

The boiler is the common system for heating water, which is then circulated around the house and heat is emitted through a variety of means. All pipework should be insulated, particularly if running through cold areas. Emitters can either be common steel radiators, which are the cheapest capital cost systems, or skirting radiators. Both these systems emit heat via a relatively low surface area and thus require water to be heated to a high temperature (around 85 degrees centigrade). Thus, fuel costs can be high. Radiators should always have reflectors behind them to the external wall otherwise a disproportionate amount of heat is lost through the wall without entering the room. Both these systems rely on convection to circulate heat, and so warm the air.

Alternative water systems include ceiling or under-floor systems, which act like large radiators. They emit radiant heat and so heat surfaces, furniture and people, which in turn heat the air.

This way a room is more evenly heated than with convection systems and has less disturbed air through fewer convection currents moving around. These systems require less fuel as the temperature of water required is much lower (around 45 to 50 degrees centigrade for under-floor systems).

While with wall radiator and warm air systems the ceilings are frequently the warmest part of the room, with under-floor heating the floor is the warmest and the ceilings the coolest. Engineers generally accept that human indoor comfort is gauged by the temperature of the feet. One of the major costs of under-floor systems is the insulation required underneath the pipework on a ground floor. If insulation is being fitted as standard, the capital cost of the remainder of the system starts to become competitive with radiator systems.

Open fires require a hole in the roof of the building to allow flue gases and heat to escape, and thus conflict with all current rationale of energy conservation. Nevertheless, open fires are very desirable and chimneys can be designed to minimise heat loss and recycle heat through heat exchangers.

The house may require a combination of heating systems, say under-floor on the ground floor, and warm air or radiators on the upper floor. Ideally, a full house energy analysis will ensure that neither system is too expensive.

The best heating systems will only be as good as the controls and energy management systems that regulate when they are in use and when not. A good control will ensure that you use only the amount of fuel you require for your comfort, with none wasted.

Good controls are multi-programmable and regulate themselves to the changing outdoor temperature as well as differing indoor requirements. Thus, economies are made both to your pocket and to the broader environment.

Appliances and light bulbs

The final area of energy conservation to consider is the efficiency of energy use of kitchen appliances and lighting.

Influences from Europe, combined with the growing tide of awareness in this country, now mean that all the major appliance suppliers see energy efficiency as a worthwhile marketing tool. Comparative research between models is the only way the most energy efficient can be found. The first Eco-labelling in this country is that of household appliances.

Compact fluorescent light bulbs are relatively new on the market and are far more expensive than normal bulbs, yet they use only a sixth of the electricity used by normal bulbs, and last much longer. Money from your VAT return should go towards their purchase.

BUILDING BIOLOGY

Building biology is the science of interactions between all life forms and the environment, and concerns the health, well-being and dignity of people within buildings.

These concerns have been ignored for many decades, where construction materials in particular have become almost entirely synthetic and unnatural, causing increasing domestic illness. Building biologists, through extensive research and testing, particularly in Germany, broadly conclude that housing should be built from natural materials, and that human beings have not adjusted, and maybe never will, to the drastic modern make-up of contemporary housing.

Building biology supports a number of key concepts useful to the individual home-builder:

- The use of breathing constructions which allow vapour to diffuse slowly through the fabric, cleansing the air by filtering out toxins, and thus delivering a form of 'natural ventilation'. For instance, timber-frame construction and cellulose insulation avoid conventional vapour barriers.
- The use of hygroscopic building materials that regulate the indoor air humidity, and are completely inert and give off no toxic vapours, eg wood.
- The use of materials that give off little or no radioactivity, and yet allow through important cosmic and terrestrial radiations, under which the human species evolved.
- Maintaining natural electrical and magnetic fields, and eliminating man-made fields.

CONCLUSION

The development brief of the ecologically minded house means venturing into all sorts of new and exciting ideas, some of which may seem obscure now, yet will be mainstream within the next century. While energy-efficient housing is the principal guiding light of the 1990s, with numerous options and solutions continually being developed to suit the individual home-builder, a broader, ecological, sustainable approach is now available for all. Green building is coming of age.

Design, if it is to be ecologically responsible and socially responsive, must dedicate itself to nature's principle of least effort . . . or doing most with least. That means consuming less, using things longer, and being frugal about recycling materials.

(Victor Papanek, *Design for the Real World*, 1985)

LIST OF ADVERTISERS

INDEX

References in italic indicate drawings.
add = address